PATRICK ROBERTSON:

A Tale Of Adventure

Brian Hennigan

Cover Artwork: Jordan Gum

ISBN: 0692539433

Brian Hennigan's business career spans many industries.

His fiction has been broadcast on BBC Radio Four and Radio Scotland.

This is his first novel.

Also by Brian Hennigan:

The Scheme of Things

For Bill and Margaret Hennigan

CONTENTS

1. PATRICK ROBERTSON

I woke at seven thirty, naked, with my right foot wedged in the top corner of the refrigerated mini-bar. Around me were scattered a variety of small bottles, all empty. Thankfully the light was off so I'd had a comparatively good night of sleep. My meeting wasn't until ten thirty and this gave me heaps of time to slap myself into condition.

Laying out of my clothes prior to bathing is one of the few untainted pleasures left. To stand at the foot of the bed, each item placed clockwise in order of dressing, with the suit jacket hanging on the back of the door like the last piece of battle armor, fills me with joy and inspiration. I breathed deeply, taking in each crease, each button, each cuff, enriching my soul with the finery of good tailoring. I laid the back of my hand gently on the soft weave of the tie. Then, taking the dressing gown firmly, I marched into the bathroom, closed the door and prepared to bathe. This took exactly thirty minutes. Same as always.

It is impossible to be completely sure that the staff in a hotel, any hotel, clean the place with absolute thoroughness. So it's best to fish a few hairs out of the plughole and place them round the place – bath, basin, bowl – so as to suggest heavy usage. This way they realize it would be just as well to give the place a good going over from the start, rather than simply polishing the odd tap.

I brushed my teeth until the gums bled, rinsing repeatedly with strong mouthwash. A hasty brush and blow-dry topped me off, finishing with a careful nostril-hair check. Putting on my clothes never takes more than three minutes, all things being equal. Standing my briefcase by the door, I put the jacket on, flipped the lights off and, without looking back, surged down to breakfast. Discipline is the key to starting each and every day well.

The week looked good on paper. I had left Taiwan with a full order book. A full order book! This hadn't happened in years. Feeling on a roll, I'd gone for it with Mr. Wong of Wong Foundries, Taipei. Few buyers understand the importance of the salesman's total sales book. Everyone thinks that the salesman must be terrified of losing each and every sale. The truth is that once an acceptable level of sales has been achieved – and this can be in financial, historical, or psychological terms – you just don't need that next one so badly. I had greeted Mr. Wong with, I believed, one of the best two-week sales-tour books that would ever be seen in Mackenzie Industries safely in my briefcase. The importance of his full-bore lathe order wasn't marginal – it was decorative.

The end was clinical. My plane departs in three hours, I had told him, and I will be on it – sale or no sale. He studied me momentarily, smiling as if sharing a joke. Within minutes we were enjoying a celebratory glass of sticky Chinese wine. Next stop Thailand and a tidy bit of business that was already, more or less, in the bag.

Thirty-six hours prior to departure my entire wardrobe had been handed in, stained or not, for cleaning, steaming, folding. Packing was an effortless ceremony of spotless sea cotton and impeccable creases. Nothing beats a good pack. A well-packed salesman can take on the world. The suitcases had been filled so that no bulge showed; each had sat straight and upright by the door. On that final night I had been manicured, shaved, styled, in the hotel beauty parlor, followed by an eye-watering massage of near-religious intensity. The night had closed in solitude on my balcony, the gentle smog of the city drifting below. I had put aside my one-liter bottle of Famous Grouse for the last night and it clouded my wandering mind beautifully. I awoke on uncrumpled linen, in ample time to shower and breakfast before the chauffeur arrived. The only moment of failure had occurred, as so often of late, when, coming to in the creamy hotel-room pallor, I was unable to say exactly which city I was in or where I was going next. I read it off the suitcase labels on the way to the bathroom.

I now despise airports. Nervous tourists, all Day-Glo backpacks and fistfuls of paper, clank along carrying just the right amount of duty-free purchases. I pilot my trolley through this befuddled sea, once unknown waters but now wearily familiar. Dimly, I can recall the association of travel with pleasure. Each terminal building brings now the same feeling of flattened hope.

 Thank God for the welcoming arms of the business-class lounge, a satellite of Hotel Land in effect and a source of great comfort. At the other end – the exit doors and welcoming corridor. It's best to keep your head down. Day after day of face after face examining and then discarding you takes its toll.

Some customers offer to have a car meet me at the airport. Everyone seems to want to be friendly with suppliers nowadays. I prefer to put off the moment when our worlds meet. Besides, I'm usually gagging for alcohol and if the customer comes along for the ride the delay before satisfaction is achieved is grinding. Airports, coming or going, are probably the worst part of my job.

As soon as we were off the ground and on our way to Thailand I buzzed the air hostess. It's as well to establish your presence as soon as possible or you simply get treated like everyone else, which isn't a service level you should go through life with. Invariably they send someone back who tells you politely that until such and such a sign pings off no drinks can be served. I ordered a large vodka tonic anyway.

The five-hour flight was direct, Taiwan–Bangkok. No tedious stopovers or touchdowns. Overall I was in excellent shape. The mild drama of the Wong sale had put me in a wonderfully light mood. Patrick Robertson would be the man of the moment in our Manchester HQ. I was in the zone and looking good. By and large I had avoided drinking too much over the fortnight. Bangkok depresses me at the best of times. Hit it with the substantial body hangover common to most trips and it's all I can do to reach window height in the taxi.

Machine tools is a "What?" industry. You tell people you sell machine tools and they say "What?" I don't care. I enjoy the anonymity. If pushed, usually by some hotel bar drinker, I can explain that we make the machines that make other machines. That's usually enough. It would be terrible to have to explain more. No one ever sees fit to comment on machine tools. God help those poor salesmen who deal in consumer products, with so many opportunities for public comment. I once watched in pity as a fellow traveler, a rambunctious, podgy, moon-faced soft drink salesman, reeled and staggered his way like an aging boxer through a two-hour assault on his industry by three animated geography teachers on a school trip. A bear pit. As if it matters. As if he should care. Better off in machine tools, matey, was all I thought.

I have been a traveling salesman for twenty years and I will never be anything else. I work for a British company, Mackenzie Industries. We are a moderately successful, family-owned company. Choose your employers well. Family-owned means no quarterly demands for increased profits, no abrupt changes of management, no relentless pressure to exceed the forecasts, no hostile-takeover sleepless nights.

Within the corporate structure, moderate success is the type to aim for. Immoderate success leads to positions of greater responsibility – more pay for far more work. Happily married, with a solid base of others to impress, and I might be interested. I'd spot trends, identify new markets, make strategic proposals. Being directed by others is much better. I take some of the strain but generally ride along. It all comes down to a retirement anyway.

It was after my fourth, maybe fifth, visit that I began to find Bangkok tedious. Dozens of subsequent visits have not magnified this feeling, nor have they diluted it. Walking at night, I can wander in and out of the torrential traffic with the indifference of a local. The once "quaint" tuk-tuk three-wheeled taxis have long lost their novelty. The motorcycle taxis were enjoyable for a while, but I was glad to return to the air-conditioned interior of a Toyota. Eventually the ceaseless sex shows of Patpong became so normal I now prefer to watch the audience. Starry-eyed teenage Western boys; sweaty, suited businessmen; stiff, liberal young couples. It never changes.

Arriving late, I had taken dinner at ten: a nondescript, other than perhaps "fiery," amalgam of vegetables. I ate as much as I could. Being neatly filled with any food is a pleasurable state. Declining dessert I headed for the bar and a large J&B. I've drunk J&B ever since noticing its preponderance in American films. If it's good enough for Hollywood film stars, it's good enough for me. I am the joyful victim of such manipulation – it adds to the agreeable, conveyor-belt feeling. Perhaps the Americans like all the royal warrants on the label. They themselves are proscribed from being royal and hence enjoy that sort of thing. And they do make all the best films.

The bar held a typically disgusting confection of people you would not wish to meet under any circumstance, least of all when traveling, alone and vulnerable. Despite the luxury prices, hotel bars are never the best filters. In the darkest corner, lit by a solitary glowing palm tree, sat one particularly repellent person.

His hair was deliberately untidy; a careful one day too long unwashed, two days unshaven. The patchwork jeans were standard fare, as was the "Hong Kong 1997 – I Was There" faded white T-shirt. A tin of tobacco sat on the table next to his room key. He looked up briefly, taking in the plush surroundings, smiling to himself. The accessibility of a place like this, to someone dressed as he, was the source of his pleasure. Such tired juxtapositioning is the mainstay of countless tedious conversations on the subject of "my year out."

I eased softly closer to see if I could actually smell him. He was plainly a hippie, and I've been looking for some time now to justify the generalization "bloody smelly hippie." Truth, especially in insults, is all. This hippie had a detailed map of South-east Asia laid out before him. He was drinking what looked like water, which is enough to put me off anyone. On the map of Asia was marked a long route in red pen – whether this was a plan or history was not clear. In the top surrounding margin was written "The Long and Winding Road – Felix!" I watched from behind a bamboo screen. The hippie reached down into his sock and removed a small black wallet. From this he fished out a gold American Express card. One of them. No chance of him being smelly.

I sat down at the bar, placing myself far from the crowd but conveniently close to the toilets, and ordered more whisky. I thought again about taking up smoking. Smokers always look more stylish when alone than non-smokers. You don't even need to inhale, just sigh pensively. I decided to start smoking. Making decisions is always enjoyable. But what brand? I thought to consult the barman and was raising my hand to attract his attention when I felt another hand on my shoulder. I turned around to find a blonde woman of perhaps thirty-five years, pleasantly tanned and slightly plump in a schoolgirlish way. Her wide-eyed expression suggested she had got the wrong person and this was soon confirmed.

"My goodness! I, um, I was looking for . . ."

"For someone else?" I offered helpfully, smiling with genuine charm.

"Yes, for someone else. I'm most sorry."

"Robertson. Patrick Robertson." I extended my hand. "No apologies necessary, my dear. Is there anything I can do for you?"

I always like to help women wherever and whenever possible. Men can piss off.

"Oh no, that's quite all right. I'm sorry."

She turned succinctly and walked off towards the lobby. It hadn't taken her long to regain her composure. Leaving the bar she turned and seemed to give a slight smile, tilting her head to one side.

There it was! That slight glow, dimly recognized, of having been favored with the affection of a nice woman. Steadying myself on the bar, I ordered another double.

What is the appropriate response to unexpected, unsolicited moments of beauty? More often than not these sudden gifts cause so much bitter reflection on their previous absence that the immediate wonder of the spectacle is eclipsed.

Pondering this question I finished up and went to my room and the waiting mini-bar, forgetting entirely to take up smoking.

2. MEETINGS

The breakfast room was still full and I was forced to share a table with two male French tourists in their mid-forties, who sat relishing their native tongue over endless coffees. There is only one thing worse than listening to the French wringing the most out of their every vowel, and that is listening to non-French people attempting the same. How many times have I sat there, my every sense organ anticipating the arrival of the brandy, only to have this carefully weighted anticipation ruined by a couple of pretentious chumps who have discovered a smattering of French in common. The usual route proceeds from either "croissant" or "chateau" and then down, down into the valley of vile inconsequence.

They continued their enunciation-fest with vigor. I read my papers. At a quarter past nine I went down to reception and ordered my taxi, giving written address details to the hotel clerk so that he might confirm them with the driver. As I waited for everything to be fixed up, the hippie from the bar came down the stairs arm-in-arm with a similarly-styled female. Seeing them descend reminded me of my ex-wife, who used to make a big thing about coming down the stairs together. "You never know when there might be a camera," she used to say, and thus we would glide gracefully down to lobby after lobby, grinning like naughty goblins, she gesturing with authority at whatever piece of mincey artwork happened to be on hand. My job was to nod. I presume this is a ritual still going on somewhere.

The male and female hippie couple had about them that amazing sense of couplehood that few couples ever attain. As they walked they turned and looked at each other, smiling in absolute self-contained smugness. Her T-shirt read 'Twin Cities Weekend of Joy," with a picture of a bug-eyed penguin. They regarded their surroundings with ill-disguised toleration.

The taxi came promptly and I left in excellent time for my appointment. Nevertheless, it was an intensely hot day and my temple was throbbing like a wound. I leant forwards in the seat, cradling my head in both hands, rocking back and forth. This never helps, but what else is there to do?

Keemcho and Son is one of innumerable medium-sized companies that have sprung up all over Thailand. The number of small- to medium-sized companies in a country is one of the determining factors that guides our sales and marketing activities – the more the better. Southeast Asia, with its Confucian heritage and new prosperity, is still awash with family-run businesses. A family-run, medium-sized company is the easiest sale in the book. They are often short on capital and consequently do a fair amount of research into potential purchases. The chances are that, if they call, they've already decided. This changes my job from a tiring "sell" into a simple "order take." I still keep a few special offers up my sleeve should the signature be a bit long in coming.

The father and son stood waiting by the gate, solidly dressed in light, green cottons. I shook their hands firmly and we went into the compound.

The rigmarole of business meetings is the most painful of responsibilities, the most exciting of activities. Each performance, each buildup to a sale is a period of intense self-loathing until that magic point when the fever kicks in and the romp to the finish begins. Maintaining one's posture until the romp begins is the grip one must never lose.

Explaining the basic position, the starting point, is the winding back of the catapult. Slow, measured, confident. It is the definition of the self. At no other moment in life do I feel so actual, so in the spotlight. Every single piece of product information, my own and that of my competitors, drops into the barrel. The memory of every single meeting I have ever had surges forward. Speaking, explaining, it is possible to see the thrill of conversion on each new customer's face. It is this image that I conjure when on occasion doubt tugs me, asking me why I am going to whatever meeting I am going to.

It would nevertheless be ridiculous to expect the excitement of these moments to survive undiminished over the long run. Indeed, it is now difficult to remember the first time that I came to in the middle of a sales pitch, wondering what the fuck I had done wrong to end up here, now.

This meeting went exceptionally smoothly. I did all the right things well; wandered through every office expressing interest in a royal manner; treated each and every employee like a rediscovered sister; agreed that everything nowadays was so expensive. When eventually we sat down I had already mapped out what the best route, most attractive alternatives, and likely outcomes were. We got round quickly to agreeing the price on a new turbine lathe and the sale was secured on the basis of a familiar story. Six months from now I would call again, and all being fine they would receive a small cooling unit at 40 percent knockdown. This offer was well received and I was spared the indignity of a reduction on the price of the first unit. Never reduce the first unit price! To make things even better they declined my offer of dinner that night. When people are spending in excess of £100,000 on one piece of machinery you expect them to take whatever else is up for grabs. Still, all the more for me.

I left them waving at the gates. A sad-looking Alsatian mongrel ran after the taxi for about half a mile, barking wildly, before being distracted by an open-air market. My head had started to throb again.

At the hotel I headed straight for my room and phoned down for a bottle of champagne. Thankfully they had some Taittinger. I then ran a bath and lathered up to shave. The bath had just reached the top when there was a sharp rap at the door. The champagne was brought in by a docile-looking Thai girl, of the type much beloved by Western men on their pre- or post-marriage holidays. She sat the bucket and stand down and I indicated I'd open it myself. She bustled out, taking a quick look over her shoulder as I fiddled with the wire release. The bottle had evidently been carried with some action, for no sooner had a modicum of pressure been removed from the cork than it shot off, champagne erupting to the ceiling. I quickly placed my mouth over the stream, but my cheeks were soon filled and liquid began oozing out of my nostrils. Swallowing as best as I could, I released my grip and fell spluttering to the floor, my face awash in champagne and shaving foam.

Shaving should take place before bathing. None of this nonsense about softening the bristles while soaking in the bath when anticipating the shave to come, all the more so if you wish to drink in the bath.

By the time my face and neck were completely smooth I had about three deep cuts, which stung like blue buggery. I immediately forced myself into the slightly too hot bath, submerging for thirty seconds, up for thirty seconds and so on for five minutes. This is how to bathe like a professional. Cleaning follows.

The Japanese have bathing down to a fine art but few Westerners are up to speed. Sit on the edge of the tub. Soap all over – especially armpits and similar crevices. Take a good sponge (a travel necessity) and give the whole body a proper scrub. While doing this, let about one fifth of the water out of the bath and refill with hot water. Now lower yourself quickly into the bath and submerge and hold for as long as possible. Repeat whole process twice.

I was now feeling magnificent, egged on by a couple of miniatures from the replenished mini-bar. My head no longer throbbed, and it had been a bloody good sale. I toweled off and dressed in my casual clothes: a plain sea cotton short-sleeve shirt and light canvas trousers, both in sky blue. I had another miniature – Bacardi, I think.

There are those who counsel against an intake of alcohol either during or after a hot bath. In point of fact this is a near-perfect biochemical operation. Replacing sweated-out, watery body fluids with alcohol produces a galloping rush quite without equal. One can feel the texture of the world changing. I necked another miniature – Gordon's?

Having handed in my key I strolled out of the hotel, at ease with the world. At a small roadside stand nearby I bought a few cans, maybe six, of a nice-looking local beer. In general, packaging is a good quality indicator for alcohol.

Bangkok could never make any claim on being one of the most beautiful cities in the world. The urban planning, such as it exists, is of a type found all over Asia – haphazard, unintelligible, indifferent. The syrupy pollution doesn't help either.

Memory threw up a nice, flowery park on the east of town, and this seemed as good an idea as any. I hailed a tuk-tuk and explained as best as I could where to go. As we spluttered jerkily along I dug into my leisure bag for the Walkman.

The leisure bag is indispensable. It is my constant companion. It is the essential piece of carry-on luggage. It is everything I need.

It is a comfortably-sized leather shoulder bag packed with a range of core material. A Walkman, three sets of batteries, the *Oxford Pocket English Dictionary*, two books by (or about — I can't remember) Dostoevsky, a selection of Mozart tapes, a pewter flask containing 110-proof vodka, a floppy sun hat. The vodka is the only emergency item – never opened but reassuring to know about. The Walkman comes a close second. The social equivalent of a life vest, it can be pulled on in all manner of choppy seas to save one from drowning in dreary conversation. Particularly useful in the business-class section of most airlines. Sony has changed the world with this device and received scant thanks. Well done, Mr. Sony!

We arrived at the floral entrance to the park. Making sure the floppy sun hat was firmly pulled on, I paid and got out. Opening another beer produced that wonderful ringpull crack which can so improve any occasion. I wandered through the gates and into the greenery, happy as a child. What a marvelous evening. Music flowing through my system, exalting my every neural impulse, the world bounced in syncopation. Boys and girls whirred by in melodic rapture; passing adults, some holding hands, embodied the very spirit of the notes forged by little Amadeus.

One of the narrower paths led down to a small, lily-covered pond. I opened a beer and sat alone on a bench in the evening shade. Was I ever happier? Of course not. I sat smiling. There was nothing I wanted for. Nevertheless, after ten minutes or so I'd had enough and continued my walk. It doesn't do any good in the long term to reflect on how happy one might be.

I walked and walked, stopping only to open beer, and was fortunate to find another little stall where I could restock. Just as my legs were beginning to usher me home there was a tap on my shoulder. A familiar tap. Turning, I found the woman from the hotel bar. I immediately removed the headphones.

"Oh! Do you like Mozart?" She pointed to the earpieces, from which a tinny *Jupiter Symphony* dribbled down my shirt. I turned it off.

"Very much," I replied. "His very accessibility is too often used as a lever with which to conjure an argument of 'pretty but shallow.'"

I smiled so she wouldn't think it was a test. She was gracefully unperturbed.

"I felt I ought to stop you and apologize for last night. Truly I thought you were someone else."

"Not at all," I said, grinning with allure. "After all, it was a genuine mistake. Perhaps I should apologize for not being the person you wanted."

Then she smiled, revealing what was undoubtedly the greatest set of white teeth ever witnessed. I reeled, stunned and aghast that I should have traveled the planet for so long and not encountered a vision of such purity.

"It's funny, us two meeting by coincidence in this park," she said, so innocently that I had to bite my tongue in a vain attempt to stay in control.

"Have . . . have you been here before?" I forced out. She hesitated.

"No . . . um . . . yes, yes, but just the once."

One area of absolute difference in sexual attraction is that of hesitancy. A hesitant man is at best one level adrift of chump. A hesitant woman, replete with mild stuttering, extended pauses, word and fact fumbling, is pulling repeatedly on the trigger of sexual attraction.

At this point I, in effect, passed out, swooning into sublime intoxication from her very person.

"Shall we go on?" She indicated the path. Mesmerized, I could but follow her gentle footfall.

Elizabeth was on a tour, "Three Points in the Mystic East" (Thailand-Malaysia-Singapore), with her elderly mother. Her father, a printer, had pulled out at the last moment through pressure of work. Yes, this was her first holiday with her mother and no, she wasn't having a great time. Under these circumstances, when Elizabeth thought she'd recognized an old school friend she had excitedly approached.

We reached the park entrance and I went to get a taxi from the stand down the road. I gave Elizabeth a beer for while I was away, which she gamely opened. Here was a woman who looked like she could enjoy a beer. Was there to be no end to such delights?

Elizabeth woke me with a sharp kick to the ribs. I hauled myself up and saw the hotel. "We're back," she said tersely.

I paid the driver while she strode willfully up the steps. Reluctantly, I watched her go. I had a terrible *faux pas* sort of feeling. At the top of the stairs she appeared to exchange words with someone in the doorway. Then she turned and with an abrupt, forceful waving of the hand beckoned to me. I galloped up the stairs and was soon at her side, somewhat breathless.

"Aren't you coming?" she asked rather testily, walking quickly into the lobby.

"Yes, yes – it's just that I'm a little bit older than you."

I smiled and she sort of grinned. As we walked to reception I managed to get sufficiently ahead of her to run and ask if she'd care to have dinner. She apologized but said the she must see how her mother was. I voiced my understanding. We stood side by side in silence, waiting for our keys. Elizabeth said,

"But I'd quite fancy a drink later on, you know. Sometime after dinner."

My heart leaped. We agreed on nine thirty and I left her to go to my room. I was aware of her watching me as I climbed the stairs and felt the first stirrings of requited love in my bosom. Once out of view I raced to my room, where I immediately set about preparing another bath.

3. A DATE

I dined alone that night, with only my torrid expectations for company. I only ate at all because I was seeing Elizabeth later. Quite often I don't eat an evening meal – it interferes with the absorption of alcohol. You might as well drink grapefruit juice on a full stomach as a couple of double vodkas. The worst is when you have to go to some official dinner or company reception or whatever. At such times one has to cope not only with an ever-filling stomach but also with the need to make polite conversation.

Dinner-table conversations are a matter of some pain for the traveling British businessman. Please save me from any more pithy observations on ethnic diversity, golf courses, quality newspapers, British car productions in the Thirties and Forties, the worldwide admiration for the Queen.

Of course in Asia there is one great blessing: chopsticks. I have no time for those who suggest that Chinese or Japanese food actually tastes better when eaten with chopsticks – palpable nonsense. The real strength of chopsticks is that you don't have to put them down in order to pick up your glass. Alcohol in one hand, food in the other. Americans almost got it right when they started this thing of cutting up all the food baby-style and then proceeding with fork alone. However, they then insist that you politely keep the spare hand in your lap. What a waste of a goblet hand, what a waste.

It was a long time since I had had womanly company, and this surprising re-emergence was very pleasant. Women do think and talk about things in a different way, and it is so refreshing. I was once told that this is a patronizing thing to say and then in the next breath that the English language is a tool of male oppression. I don't like being bogged down with so much philosophy. Besides, I wasn't concerned with such stuff that night. I wanted merely to be with Elizabeth; to hold her; to worship her.

How was this accomplished? I know of two methods for impressing women: interest and disinterest. The successful combination of the two is a ticket to delight and comfort. Timing is crucial. Examples:

1.

MAN: Fancy a drink?

WOMAN: Yes please, I'll have a Cinzano and orange.

MAN: You'll be lucky.

Too dismissive, vulgar even.

2.

WOMAN: Isn't the moon big tonight?

MAN: Yes it is, my dear.

WOMAN: Do you remember that scene in *Casablanca*?

MAN: I'm going home.

Overreaction. End of story.

3.

MAN: Shall we go to the cinema?

WOMAN: Yes, let's.

MAN: Perhaps it's not such a good idea.

This latter course allows the man to discover the female interest in films without any form of commitment. He demonstrates to the female that he is of opinion and character, someone to whom life is but a plaything; a fancy; a mere bagatelle.

 Not all women take to this method of relationship-building. The form is still in its infancy, so it must be delivered with something of a pioneering spirit. The easy option would be to go back to the traditional ways of wooing. I prefer to break the mold. On such journeys resistance is inevitable.

I mulled these thoughts over as, by regular mouthfuls, the dinner before me diminished. The food was tasteless and gratifyingly undemanding. If only this were more often the case. I finished with a dessert of fruit cake with cream and, high on the sweetness, made off to the bar downstairs.

The Bamboo Garden was crowded, packed. On previous visits I had never seen the place more than half-full. A dress code was in operation – smart – meaning jacket and tie. Every jacket bore a lapel badge. I was in a conference bar. Around me were perhaps hundreds of people gathered for some arcane business forum.

 Contemplating how best to get through, I was set upon by the company newcomer whose job it inevitably is to issue lapel badges. He was desperate to pin something on me.

 "And you are . . . ?" he urged.

 "I am Patrick Robertson," I declared.

 "Oh, Mr. Robertson. Excuse me." He began riffling frantically in his box of badges.

"I won't need one of those," I said, and eased past him and away.

I had to take care not to catch anyone's eye on the way to the bar, lest I be seized on by some would-be colleague. Already my mood was black. I dislike the false camaraderie of business people in general. Give them a few drinks and you would think that they were doing something moral, such is their conviction.

I kept my head down, though even then I could detect that only inches from me were assorted youngsters hoping for introductions. I held to my dead reckoning and was soon able to lay one hand on the smooth marble counter. Most of the people were drinking see-throughs of one type or another – gin mostly, I imagined. There was a need to mark my territory.

"A large Bloody Mary, please," I announced with some satisfaction. I raced it down and reloaded double-quick. Elizabeth would arrive at any moment. Get my lines in order! I turned, glass to mouth, to watch the entrance. It was rather difficult to see across the heaving masses. Straining to do so I was snagged by a doe-eyed junior with an opening gambit of "Ah, Mr. Sinclair, I was hoping I might meet you." I looked down at him reproachfully and muttered something terse in German. Just then Elizabeth appeared. Dressed simply in a dark green short-sleeve blouse with white culottes, her face was a perfect smile.

"Hello, how are you?" she asked sweetly.

"Fine, thanks. And you? I think we're in a conference bar, by the way," I nodded at those around us.

"Mm, it's so crowded – shall we go somewhere else?"

What a brilliant mind! I suggested a small bar across the road and down a bit, and Elizabeth felt this would be fine. We negotiated our way through the crowd and out of the hotel, walking down the street in excitingly close proximity. The evening air was deliciously cool and I was feeling fresh and worthy. Alive in that raw vitality only encountered when one heart was found another. Alive to life and oneself completely.

"How often do you come to Bangkok?" she asked.

"Oh, whenever Bangkok needs me," I said nonchalantly, smiling deeply. Elizabeth acknowledged my wit and senior position with a gentle flutter of her eyelids.

We crossed the road to reach the Metal Petal Lounge, only just avoiding death beneath the wheels of some bloody jeep-type machine that careered round the corner with no care or attention. I reacted instinctively, pushing Elizabeth to safety, then rounding with passion on the car as it sped off, managing a quick gesticulation before it disappeared. I ran to Elizabeth and asked if she was all right. She managed a sort of squeak and I thanked God loudly, twice. We proceeded into the safety of the bar, pausing only momentarily while I apologized to the fruit stall owner whose goods Elizabeth had scattered when she had ploughed into his cart at some speed.

The interior of the bar was much more to my liking – plain and empty – and I knew instinctively that the evening was going to go well. I bade Elizabeth sit down at a small table and asked her what she would like to drink.

"Hmmh, could I have a gin martini, please?"

I seized the moment – "Of course not, but then again, why shouldn't you?" – and turned quickly on my heel for the counter. I felt that I had hit the interest/disinterest equation plumb on the head. Returning with our drinks I found, however, that Elizabeth was clearly still upset about the jeep, and I worked quickly to calm her.

"Don't worry, Elizabeth." I reached for her hand. "Those evil men will probably be wiped out at the next junction."

She faced me in a rather aggressive manner, and I sensed mild disapproval. I released her hand and urged her to take a drink, which she did with relish. I glanced at the ceiling – watching women noisily gulp down strong alcohol isn't polite.

The evening had not had an auspicious start, but it soon began to reveal its hidden treasure. Elizabeth regained composure after her fourth gin martini, and I was definitely much improved on my earlier sober self. We joked and laughed on various subjects. I continued to implement the interest/disinterest strategy, content that my aim was true. Elizabeth was definitely taken with me.

It was shortly after eleven. I was concluding the amusing tale of the time that I and a fellow guest had, to great effect, put blue dye into the industrial washing machine at the Hong Kong Peninsular on account of their poor room service performance. Elizabeth finished laughing and said,

"I think it's time we went home, don't you?"

I felt my pulse quicken.

"Yes, I do, I do."

Together we rose and gathered ourselves for an exit. The place was still empty but now possessed a magical ambience quite absent on our arrival. A friendly wave to the barman, and we began the short walk back.

The road was crossed with care, Elizabeth insisting that I go first. As we neared the hotel my mind was overtaken by so many thoughts. Principal among these was, would those dear lips be willing to accept mine? I tripped going up the steps, and Elizabeth steadied my fall. Standing close together in the moonlight I could hear her breathing, my heart alive to its gentle release. She brushed the hair from her forehead and looked at me pointedly.

"Would you like to see me to my room?"

"Of course, Elizabeth, it would be a pleasure."

Women can be so very difficult about this sort of thing, dragging it out interminably. First you see them to your door, then along the street, then up the road, then to their gate, then up to their door. What is needed is a formalized leave-taking ceremony. Something like,

MAN: Now you go.

WOMAN: Yes, I do.

The two then kiss goodnight.

So much of the wonderful ritual of life has been destroyed by the modern, ridiculous infatuation with being constantly original, different. The Japanese have a saying: "There is ceremony even between the closest of friends." Such concepts have been lost to us, and as a result so are we.

The hotel was quite still. From the bar came the sounds of stragglers and lower ranks, long past hovering around for introductions and now intent on "a night to remember." We started up the dimly-lit stairs.

"Which floor are you on?" I asked without trying to sound too interested (not easy).

"The fifth, 519."

I wished we'd taken the elevator. My mind jumped to a forgotten element.

"Will your mother still be awake?"

Elizabeth stopped, not entirely certain, hesitating.

"Yes, she may be. We'd better go quietly."

It struck me that I didn't know or couldn't remember Elizabeth's surname, and that this could prove awkward if the mother was still up.

"Elizabeth, what's your family name, please?" I asked.

"Rawson, Elizabeth Rawson."

We reached the fifth floor and Elizabeth moved off to the left, taking the key out of her handbag. She jangled this rather loudly and I had a good mind to take it off her and demonstrate how keys could be held quietly, but I know how offended women get at the slightest suggestion that they are technically illiterate. I was also completely out of breath and could barely keep up anyway. Nevertheless, Elizabeth was making a fearful amount of noise as we approached room 519, walking with a stern, thumping gait. I decide that I really didn't want to meet her mother and with enormous effort overtook, getting to the door and placing myself between her and the lock.

"Elizabeth, I must go now. Shall I see you tomorrow?"

She seemed extremely agitated by this sudden action on my part, and I sensed my chances of a fond kiss goodnight diminishing.

"Yes, yes of course you will . . . but . . . wait just a minute," and with a fast movement of her hand she rapped three times on the door. What lunacy was this? I was by now quite resolved that I did not wish to meet her mother and angry at this blatant attempt to rouse her. I was staring in puzzlement at Elizabeth when suddenly the door was pulled open. Instinctively my politeness leapt into action and I turned, half bowing, to the doorway.

"Mrs. Rawson, delighted to meet you, I was just vouchsafing your charming daughter's return."

I was expecting some sort of grumpy reply. What I did not expect was the excited yelp of "Ha!" that greeted me. Nor the pillowcase that was thrust violently over my head. There was a sharp shove from behind, and I fell startled and confused into the room.

4. SURPRISE

I awoke screaming. So at first it was as if nothing had happened; as if this were just another morning in some nice luxury hotel somewhere. Occasionally, after a bout of pre-consciousness screaming, I have bumped into the occupant of the neighboring room. Generally speaking this is a fellow businessman and it is an unwritten code of honor that the appropriate greeting on such occasions as a curt "Good morning." Life on the road can be tough and all salesman soon grow used to early-morning cries of anguish.

But as vision returned I was able to take in the four figures standing over my quivering, prostrate form and I realized that I was now far removed from the comfort of corporate anonymity. All around was the rich, lush green of the jungle. To my immediate left was a well-turned-out bearded man with spectacles and floppy white hat; to his left Elizabeth, and to the right of me stood the self-righteous, smiling figures of the two hotel hippies. The old enemy itself. Screaming, I collapsed back into darkness.

I have never liked surprises. Least of all those involving Other People. The concept of the unexpected personal appearance – perhaps of a work colleague, university acquaintance or offspring – as a pleasurable thing has always eluded me. Not that this happens often any more. A surprise party for me to celebrate twenty years with the company was an ideal opportunity to demonstrate my unsuitability for such events. I had been requested to attend an urgent, unscheduled Strategy Review in Manchester. I entered the appropriate hotel meeting room having come directly from the airport after a twelve-hour flight. As such I was still sobering up. Fifty or so company employees, garbed for fun in recklessly cheerful blouses and shirts, shouted "Surprise!'" and burst into "For He's a Jolly Good Fellow." There was little that could be done immediately. I accepted a couple of toasts, the three-piece, middle-aged band started and I slipped out and booked myself on the next available flight back. I then drank myself stupid until the time came to depart. As the last gaggle of staff were hokey-cokeying around the hotel foyer, I broke into the MD's suite and laid an enormous shit on his pillow. Forty minutes later I was on my way back to Jakarta. A fax the next day apologized for the early departure, noting candidly that the conspicuous absence of my (recently ex-) family was too much. Meanwhile the shit had provided the right amount of distraction. Someone was sacked, I recall. There have been no similar gatherings since.

The family does not hold surprise parties for me either. However, I understand, from a misaddressed invite a couple of years ago, that there is an annual bash to celebrate the divorce.

Slap, poke. Slap, slap, slap. Tweak. I felt myself being assailed by various hands and came to fending them off. The bearded man and the female hippie were administering these stimuli. Spluttering, I demanded they stop and, seeing me fully conscious, they desisted. The bearded man helped me to my feet and then extended his hand. Immediately my own shot out in reflex salesman action.

There is no doubt that should hell turn itself inside out and the putrid bodies of so many of the world's worst rise from the deep and stride forth; should a reanimated Attila and his massed hordes comes thundering over the plains, there would appear from the terrified nations a equal army of salesmen. To meet them; to greet them; to shake their hands. There is nothing we do so well and no one can beat us at it. Salesmen are at their most magnificent at that first moment of contact. The customer conversion process is ignited there and then. Where else in all of human life can one experience such raw fire? It is perhaps inevitable, therefore, that a general malaise descends soon after, for how can subsequent discussion possibly live up to the initial spiritual promise? Wedding receptions can be the scene of the most dreadful pornographic displays, with the deeply upsetting receiving-line ritual. When attendance at such affairs was an unavoidable aspect of being married to someone, I would nevertheless refuse to take part. For such shallow events a simple nod, I feel, suffices.

The bearded man said softly,

"Mr. Robertson – pleased to meet you. My name is Roger Hunterston. Sorry that it had to be this way."

Everything about Roger Hunterston emanated reason, purpose, and control. But not in the strident, demonstrative way normally associated with some of my stroppy business colleagues. He was a tidy man with a tidy beard, neither tall nor short, fat nor thin. In every respect he looked reasonable. A short-sleeved white shirt was tucked neatly into knee-length, multi-pocketed khaki shorts. Clean, white socks tipped just so much out of the well-worn hiking boots. Quiet, unambiguous, solid intent. He smiled, completely at ease.

"What is going on?" I eventually managed.

"Oh." He smiled, hesitating in an engaging fashion which would give all those he addressed the feeling that they were worthy of deep consideration. "You've been kidnapped. Would you like some tea?"

He dropped my hand and before I knew it the male hippie had thrust a mug of strong, hot tea into it. I became aware of the small picnic that had been arranged, with a camping stove, kettle, and assorted accessories. In the corner of the clearing was an old Peugeot delivery van, presumably what had got us here, wherever here was.

"Hello, I'm Paul," the hippie said, bowing with slight, condescending diffidence. "And this is Sally," he continued, indicating his companion, who smiled happily. "You know Elizabeth, don't you?" he asked.

Elizabeth stood off to his left, kicking the ground in a slight, petulant manner. Her white canvas trousers were mucky-looking, while a blue sweatshirt was inappropriately thick and soaked in sweat. I raised a hand in gentle acknowledgment. She raised a single finger. "Dirty Conglomerate Pig!" she spat out.

I stood, trying to take everything in.

"I think it would be good if we were to explain ourselves." Roger was addressing his team rather than me, motioning with his hands for them to gather round and be seated. In so doing they had the air of a group of schoolchildren, eager to please their teacher. Roger indicated for me to join them, cross-legged on the ground. Roger himself then sat down and asked if everyone was comfortable. Then he looked at me. "Now then."

Collective creativity, particularly when practiced by a group of ambitious yet dull minds, is a seriously pathetic thing. I was in the hands of the People's Earth Friendly Liberation Group. Clearly each of the four had insisted on one word or other. Such team-based compositions are made all the worse when there is a desire to make the moral goal of the enterprise an intrinsic part of the title. The corporate world does not resonate to the echo of Good-Intentioned This or Well-Meaning That. And with reason. Business needs simple definition. Consider the desolate beauty of company names such as 3M, Shell, Motorola, Gestetner, Schlumberger, National Semiconductor. Here is clarity. Here is purpose.

If bad copywriting had been their sole distinguishing feature then the situation might have been bearable. A short period of captivity, properly fed and watered, with some lively business types seeking to extort several millions from Mackenzie Industries, might have been a pleasant way to spend a week or two. At least my talents would have been appreciated. Their name gave it away, though. They had "good intentions" and I was therefore never likely to score highly, on whatever scale they constructed.

Roger Hunterston was a biologist. He intimated that those around were part of his organization. He was one of those men who think directness a vulgarity used only by the unintelligent. Words dripped ponderously from his lips like water from a leaky tap. This all came out over several cups of tea. Roger had all of his team do bits of the explanation, something in which they were clearly well-drilled. The background of the captors themselves was distinctly unpleasant. Apart from Roger all had been in various states of traveling the world immediately prior to this "necessary action." The hotel duo, Paul Hippie and Sally Hippie – I was never to learn their surnames – had spent over three years wandering around Southeast Asia; Indonesia and Malaysia for the most part. There was no mention of any work and I recalled the American Express card. Rich, indulgent parents are responsible for so much tatty youth.

Elizabeth had been living and working in Hong Kong, most likely as an English teacher, although this was never confirmed. Certainly an English teacher is likely. It would account for the perceptible chip on her shoulder and her desire to "do something." English-language teachers living abroad inevitably end up with savagely jaundiced views of the world. In particular they resent the fact that, despite their clear ability to understand and explain their host culture better than the natives, all anybody ever wants to do with them is practice English. And if they have occasion to return home, to go back to the old country, nobody takes them seriously anyway. Elizabeth was probably a Late Seizer, one of those who are suddenly infused with the phrase *"Carpe Diem"* – "Seize the Day." These people are abruptly possessed by the need to "do something." Generally they prove completely arrogant, ill-prepared and, most importantly, ineffective. Always avoid those you might suspect of being a Late Seizer. I had stupidly allowed myself to be duped by one.

Their link was the environment; a common desire to "make a difference." Roger had recruited them in some way or other, I suspected through the network of cheap backpacker accommodations dotted around all major Asian cities.

The logic of their stated position was simple. Every day countless thousands of trees, plants, animals, and so forth, "the magical, biological lifeblood of the planet," were being destroyed. This gorging of the world's resources was entirely unnecessary. With minimal planning and coordination it was more than possible to satisfy global resource requirements on a sustainable basis.

"All of this is incontrovertible," Roger noted sanguinely. The others sighed wearily, almost in self-pity, as if the burden of knowledge was theirs alone. "No one disputes these facts. But equally no one will do anything about it."

I nodded in agreement. Complete understanding coupled with complete inaction is familiar territory to anyone of a corporate background.

"The world is suffering from what I call 'destruction creep,'" Roger affirmed. He paused that I might ask enquiringly, "Destruction creep?" I obliged.

"Destruction creep. Consider the vast swathes of forest lost every year. Imagine if, instead of being done in so many thousand daily truckloads, these forests were to disappear overnight, as if by magic. The shock would be global, the outcry immense. Something would be done then!"

I looked from face to face around the acolytes, all of whom were receiving this mantra with total glee. I might as well not have been there.

"But destruction creep means that, instead, there is this daily frittering away, this gnawing at the edges. The gradual creep of destruction is noticed but it is insufficient to shock. Without shock there is no compelling reason to alter activity."

This last observation would be recognizable to students of negotiation. It is called Russian Front. The name comes from the exhortation given to German soldiers when faced with unpopular tasks. They would be informed, "Either you carry out this action or you'll be sent to the Russian Front." Staying in the Manila Hilton, I invented a cocktail called Russian Front – five parts Stolichnaya vodka floating on two parts blue curaçao After a couple of these one is equally willing to do anything.

"What we're doing now is, reluctantly, taking the matter into our own hands," Roger explained with intense, soft persuasion as I sucked at my plastic cup.

"Kidnapping is not something any of us would ordinarily consider. But what options do we have? The complicity of the machinery of First-World organizations in this ongoing, mindless wasting process is inescapable."

"Exploitative, First-World filth!" Elizabeth boiled over. Paul and Sally maintained their smiles. All four seemed unaware of the rivulets of sweat running off the ends of their noses. Roger continued,

"None of us are unreasonable people; indeed it is because of our extreme reasonableness that we find it necessary to take what some people might consider at best criminal and at worst terrorist steps. Do you understand, Mr. Robertson?"

I nodded slowly, then asked, the words gathering pace as I found my voice, "But why have you picked on me? Why *me*?

What do you hope to achieve by kidnapping me? What on earth?"

I felt my composure slipping and tried to calm myself down. Roger looked at me and shook his head with resignation.

"I'm afraid the answer has to be 'Nothing.'"

"Nothing?" I asked. He nodded.

"You mean to tell me you hope to achieve nothing by kidnapping me? That there is no point to this whatsoever?" I stood up, becoming quite agitated.

"No, I'm afraid not. You see, we've kidnapped the wrong Patrick Robertson."

Shock. Full frontal shock. Then a tremendous bolt of anger. To be kidnapped is bad enough, but to find that you are not in fact the person they want is to be doubly humiliated. Throughout their explanation a part of my mind had been turned to an examination of my pedigree for being kidnapped. This brief study of past form had managed to construct a vision of my life that established me as a fairly justifiable target. The sale of twenty chainsaws to that pig farmer in South Korea, chanced upon in a hostess bar, had been recast as a major piece of environmental larceny; the extension of credit terms to a paint manufacturer in Kuala Lumpur could be seen as a significant finger on the scales of ecological balance. Why wouldn't an environmental action group target me? Abruptly, this life of important crimes was over. The farmer in South Korea was simply the schmuck I'd taken him for; the paint manufacturer but one bright morning's happy gift horse. I was instantly deflated. For a moment I had glimpsed a life of consequence, a life of meaning, only to have had it snatched away. Just then I could not possibly have imagined that there was worse to come. But there was.

5. THE LAST OF MANY

My captors covered the van in camouflage netting and we set off on foot, already sodden with sweat simply through sitting. Roger, however, continued to look cool and composed. Looking cool and composed is an essential part of building a reputation. The key is how you react in an emergency or crisis. For example:

SALES DIRECTOR: Your biggest customer has just gone bust. We need to re-assign his orders by 5 p.m. or the Board will have us tarred and feathered.

SALESMAN: Oh God! We're doomed!

Wrong. Right:

SALESMAN: I think that that photocopier is playing up again. Anyone seen my car keys?

For both responses the actions ultimately taken and the likely outcome will be the same. But the impression created is completely different.

I was handcuffed to Paul Hippie, something for which there was no end of apology. "We really don't want to do any of this," crooned reasonable Roger. At no point was physical violence offered but I felt no doubt that, despite the airy-fairy intent of the group, it would be if required. I was positioned with firm hands. There was an unmistakable air of training having taken place. All movements were controlled, precise, practiced.

About one hour later we arrived, soaked through, at a large man-made clearing. A small wooden hut stood alone in the shade. Roger and Elizabeth went into the hut and emerged a few moments later with a handcuffed and manacled trio. Three depressed men, of about thirty, forty and sixty years, shuffled forwards. They regarded me with indifference. "Not another," said the eldest. The other two looked at each other, then down at the ground. The youngest was an architect, the second a computer programmer, the oldest a retired baker. They were all Patrick Robertson.

The retired baker had been first, caught while sleazing his way round the Bangkok red-light district. The circumstance of his capture clearly embarrassed him. If perverts were more up front half their problems would be over. One minute he's ambling hopefully down an alley towards a "Hello for Little Boys" sign, the next he's bundled into a plastic sheet by middle-class hoodlums.

The architect had followed shortly after. He'd just come from a meeting with clients, agreeing the final décor for an upmarket apartment block. Entering the hotel lift, he was tipped into a laundry basket. Rather sadly the gang had realized almost immediately that he was the wrong man and, not wanting the police on their back, they'd forged a postcard to his wife explaining everything; that he'd fallen in love with a hooker and was going to live with her in a commune on one of the islands off the southwest coast. The postcard had asked that the wife take good care of the children, adding pointedly that a correct attitude to the environment should be instilled from an early age.

The computer programmer had been got through a simple lure into an apparently normal taxi. It wasn't until the taxi had started bouncing through streams in the jungle, and the driver had been joined by a brother who insisted on sitting in the back, that the computer programmer had become suspicious. He'd pressed them on how far it was to the airport and it was then that they had hit him over the head. So now they had four Patrick Robertsons. A set. A hand. A bravado.

The real Patrick Robertson is a Vice-Director of the International Monetary Fund (Development Economics Division), who had been expected in Bangkok for a session with local credit unions on prudent lending. The mistaken identity issue was quite understandable. If one considers the ten largest companies in the world, or the top five international organizations, it is highly unlikely that the average person could name even the chairman, let alone any of the board members. For all the power and influence these positions command, the operators are largely unknown. Local towns, communities, nay, whole countries can be devastated economically on the basis of a single commercial decision. This would be much more difficult to accomplish if the main players were immediately recognizable figures. Granted there are, globally, one or two well-known business faces at any moment. But these few are generally mission-minded intruders, clever types who have happened upon a good idea and then milked it for all it's worth – not real "sell anything" entrepreneurs.

Thus when the group learned of the forthcoming visit of Patrick Robertson, it would have been from the smallest of paragraphs, on the most pictureless of newspaper pages. With only a name to go by, what else could be expected? Their only good fortune had been to have had Bangkok as the scene of the crime. Things happen to people in Bangkok, particularly Western males. Most of the girls looking for Western wedding fodder are not even Thai – the Philippines is by far the largest supplier of the idealized, complaint Oriental bride. The number of British or German or American husbands who discover their true love in the form of a diminutive, obedient figure who can't communicate verbally is illustrative of what your average male in such cases means when they plead, "I feel she understands me so much more." The relevant embassy is left with the weary task of explaining to tear-stained, middle-aged Western housewives why the police do not feel there is any case to answer. So, in our case, it was highly unlikely that any serious digging would be done for months and by then there would be more dust than trail.

Roger got food preparations under way and then spoke to us Patricks, explaining that, while they were sorry about the mistakes that had been made, it was now the case that they had to cope with what they had. As he put it, the tools were different but the job was the same. They were at this point "reformulating their strategy" to "take advantage of the present status."

It is sickening, the persona and jargons that people will adopt to try and cloak themselves in authority. For myself I can remember how intoxicated I was with the phrase "We have ignition," as used by the NASA countdown man immediately prior to the 3-2-1 sequence. Realizing that I would never work for NASA, I waited until I got my own vehicle before using it. It was not really my vehicle. In order to get away from my parents I had volunteered at nights to drive clumps of old people to bingo in the council minibus. Dull maybe, but I nevertheless insisted that, once the last one had been hoisted abroad, I would turn the key crisply and announce, "We have ignition." Unfortunately on my fourth night this was misinterpreted by one passenger as meaning that the minibus was on fire, and she jettisoned herself at a pedestrian crossing.

These kidnappers were no different from my youthful self. Things were "securized," items "unavailabled," food stores "accuratized." The young must have their fun, I thought. Only too soon will they realize the limits that our specified parcel of language places on minds and worlds.

In linguistic terms the one phrase that ought to be learnt in the language of whichever country you visit is "What a load of nonsense you talk." It's a great conversation finisher. And turning your back on someone means the same in every culture. Most people spend their lives looking for conversation starters. Why?

My first meal in captivity, my first meal as one of a troupe of Patrick Robertsons, was rather grim. Apart from breakfasts, where it is unseemly, I could not remember the last occasion when I had eaten a meal without alcohol. Everyone else appeared content with the mild offering of lentil curry and bread, washed down with warm, purified water. This would have been enough for me too had there been as little as a couple of glasses of literally any wine to wash it down with. I thought ruefully of all those countless little airline bottles, even one would have been enough.

Prior to being bedded down we were informed that "the plan" would be explained to all of us the following morning. That there were to be no further attempts on Patrick Robertsons was made immediately clear. Evidently they had enough. Roger noted in closing that we should not entertain any false hopes of an early reunion with our loved ones. "Far better to work with us towards our common goal than to try and force any issue," he explained. This was not such a big thing for me as I don't have any loved ones. I don't believe in them; they clutter your life and are forever trying to stop you drinking.

We Patricks had our hands and feet tied together once we were lying on the ground, with one captor positioned next to each of us.

"It's just a precaution," explained Roger. "As much for your own safety as for ours."

Elizabeth lay next to me. I smiled at her and she bent and checked my bindings warily. "Despicable business scum," she hissed. Dirty, sweaty, sticky, I could hardly argue. Her own unwashed state was probably affecting her tolerance. I asked her what she thought was going to happen tomorrow, but she simply ignored me.

So it was that I came to later that night looking up at the canopy of the jungle, lying next to someone who, at least that night, didn't seem to like me much. Mackenzie Industries was no more than a faraway dream. Before I knew it saliva was dribbling forth and even as I moved to prevent it running down my cheeks I was drowned in an orgiastic desire to have a fruity red wine running over, through and around my lips, my fingers, my body, flooding my very soul. It must have been fully another hour before I drifted back to sleep again. By this time the wine had changed to a rich, oaky Australian Chardonnay. It goes well with duck.

6. MISSION

There are forty stages to the dawn. Normally I sleep through all of them. But occasionally, when either the drinking has been prolonged or the hangover starts with such prompt severity that sleep is impossible, I will watch for each stage and try to remember when I first noticed this phenomenon. This exercise is impossible in airplanes. On one occasion (possibly Manila-Guangzhou) I felt positive that I had caught the fifteenth stage and raced round the business-class cabin, waking my fellow passengers so that they might join the vigil. There followed a brisk chase up and down the length of the plane, the crew intent on reseating me while I, vigil long-forgotten, snatched what drinks I could from the seat-top trays in economy class.

The atmosphere in the morning light resembled that of a school outing. Roger was nowhere to be seen. His absence created an expectant air, that of nervous piglets awaiting the farmer. He appeared from the bushes quite suddenly, to audible gasps from the rest of the company. It was clear to me that he had been standing there for some time before revealing himself. It is always good to stop and gather oneself for a couple of seconds before entering a room, then sweep the door open in a single move and stride in. This looks so much more decisive in appearance than simply walking in without pause. Don't ask me why. At any rate the way Roger swept through the bush made me think of someone who practices making an entrance. He stood in the clearing as certainly as a conductor on the podium.

"Friends, I have given our situation some thought, and I believe I have arrived at an acceptable answer to the current circumstances."

I nodded positively before noticing that he seemed to be excluding us Patricks – hands still tied, sitting on the ground – from his address.

"Our position in practical terms is made more difficult by our failure to capture the real Patrick Robertson. Our moral position is undiminished nevertheless. It is simply a case of adapting the resources to fit our purpose."

With a slight, open-palm movement he indicated the four of us. As the captors turned to look I smiled benevolently to indicate that I was a willing, complacent and by no means troublesome resource. Elizabeth seemed to bare her teeth at me, even to growl. To have such a fetid passion for any cause cannot possibly be a good thing.

Roger was, of course, using the concentric-rings-of-loyalty system of communication. First he would bond the inner group into a tightly-knit core; then, I imagined, he would involve us in a second ring of responsibilities and communications. Each ring supports the other, with the aim of driving forward the central goal. I know all this because, in the days when Mackenzie Industries was still trying to promote me into General Management, I had to attend a two-day seminar on the subject, for which some expert was undoubtedly paid a handsome fee. It's the type of contrivance which my father, an academic, always felt comfortable with.

"Now listen to me, you lot!" shouted a voice from the groups of Patricks; the baker. "This is a bloody outrage. Who the hell do you think you are? Let us go immediately!" This was followed by a chorus of "Quite right," "Yes!" and "Mm!" from our corner.

Roger moved towards us. His voice was quiet, firm; a mere tweak away from absolute dismissiveness. I kept my head down.

"Selfishness is such an ugly human trait. We are all in this together. We are not fighting to save our own individual planets. We are fighting for the sake of our common home, the earth. This very same earth on which every creature depends for life."

He crouched down, the fingertips of his right hand now touching the very same earth he was talking about. A master of presentation skills. You can get courses on this sort of thing but he had a smoothness to his delivery and movement which rose above any mere ten-point checklist for effective communication.

"We are here together for a reason. Our individual fates may be different but our communal heritage demands the same of us all. Now if you will be so good as to hear me out you will understand how we can all achieve the liberation we seek. You from the ropes that literally bind you, ourselves from the inner chains of guilt brought about by letting our world be destroyed."

Analogies are particularly effective in uniting apparently unconnected actions or desires. Anyone with such well-defined control of their language was not to be tackled on a whim and I decided to avoid drawing attention to myself. He turned and marched back to join the others.

"Our purpose has not been diluted; indeed its strength is beyond question. We must not let temporary setbacks unsettle our union. Are we agreed?"

They all nodded vigorously.

"I need to hear that we are together. Now tell me – are we agreed?"

"Yes, yes," they cried without reserve.

It was clever of him to get commitment in advance to an as-yet-unannounced plan. I felt that this was not all to my advantage. From the Patricks came the sound of sobbing.

Roger was not finished. To his left sat three large canvas holdalls, evidently previously hidden nearby. He explained that we would all be getting more appropriate clothing. The prospect of a change of clothing is an excellent way to excite most modern adults. How many of us do not relish the embrace of a good clean shirt, the insertion of a leg down the crease of a solid pair of trousers? The type of person who is unmoved by such sentiment is not the type that I would wish to meet.

The kidnappers set about opening the bags and laying out the contents. Roger himself untied us all rather chummily, as you might help a friend on with their overcoat, making us feel that he was doing us a favor. He explained that each person was to receive one T-shirt, one jacket, one pair of trousers, one pair of gaiters, one pair of nylon socks and one pair of boots. There would be enough to go around, he said, because they had planned for spare sizes, and he, Roger would not be taking his items – that which he had on would suffice.

The gaiters worn with nylon socks were absolutely essential, he stressed. As were the high-collared shirts. These were the items that would prevent the two kinds of leeches from getting a grip on us. The first type of leech dropped from the trees onto necks and shoulders. These were the smaller of the two; short and stubby. Our shirts, worn with some wrapped-around cloth, would protect against this first type. The gaiters tucked tight into near-indestructible nylon would stop the other type of leech that likes to crawl up your leg. These particular leeches were the largest type and could be very debilitating. The boots themselves had small holes to allow water to sluice out and sealed tongues to prevent leeches and "other things" getting inside. The combination of these design details was powerful and made us all feel very equipped. Feeling very equipped is one of the best ways to get through any day, anywhere. Finally green floppy bush hats were issued. Roger had almost redeemed himself. Then he positioned himself centrally, hands on hip, ready to speak.

"The rainforest can be a . . . a dangerous place," Roger began with a tease. We should stay close together at all times. His emphasis of "at all times" served as both warning and justification. We were to halt when told to. There was a rapid-crouching practice session. All good team-building stuff.

It was when we were going down for our third or possibly fourth emergency crouch (something to do with tree snakes) that I noticed a pile behind Roger. A small collection of luggage. At the top was my leisure bag. Salvation!

The humid air, Roger explained, would cause us problems. The abundant moisture meant that all living things were susceptible to fungus and similar growths. Athlete's foot, for example. It was therefore necessary, he continued, to check all likely areas on a regular basis. This was wherever hair grew. From then on it was possible to catch each member of the group checking out these areas. Nobody knew exactly what they were looking for. This, though, as anyone who has ever wanted a relationship could tell you, is no barrier to ceaseless activity.

Roger outlined the plan. We were to walk to a position several miles from here. There, base camp would be set up. Provisions and materials were already in place. Once properly established deep in the jungle, it would be possible to send suitable demands and threats to the powers that be and in so doing secure some measurable environmental advance in exchange for the release of the four Patricks. The original plan with the real Patrick Robertson had been to halt construction of a massive reservoir, funded in part by the IMF. Now, with just four lesser Patrick Robertsons, Roger seemed willing to compromise on some logging concessions.

Roger explained quietly that, forthwith, there would be no need to keep the Patricks tied up. "We are fairly deep into the rainforest already. With each step we minimize the likelihood of anyone finding their way out on their own."

He let this hang.

"We have the local knowledge, the rainforest know-how and the maps." He tapped his side-satchel reassuringly. "Together we have nothing to fear."

He let this hang, too.

"You should not attempt to escape. We are at least ten days' march from any civilization. Should you leave our company I am absolutely sure you will die, lost in the rainforest."

He scanned for understanding. I could not let the luggage hang one minute longer.

"Excuse me, but are those our bags?"

I pointed at the pile. Roger was not pleased at having his revelatory thunder stolen. This was disappointing. A true master of presentation is able to ride anyone's wave. The rest of the kidnappers looked apprehensively to Roger for a lead. Finally, he gave it.

"Yes, we thought it desirable that you should in some way feel at home. Please accept it as our offering of good faith."

The body Patrick launched itself forward with abandon, as monkeys on a pile of ripe bananas, hands flailing. I was no less shameful than the others, scrambling back to a leafy corner to examine the bag, shielding it from all others. The strap was soon undone and I spilled the contents on the ground. A flash of silver – the flask. Snatching, I clutched it to my bosom, laughing in delight. Turning back to the clearing, all eyes were on me.

"Sentimental value," I countered.

The group was gathered into a simple marching formation – two by two – one Patrick to each kidnapper. I was assigned to Paul Hippie. One last check was made on the camp, that all rubbish was clear and that all feces had been properly buried. We were on our way.

7. TREK

The jungle got thicker. The trees became closer together, the air less free. Looking back, an edge could be detected, with more sky and less foliage. Gradually this vanished. The sound of birdsong increased. We were all soaked in juicy sweat.

I have become accustomed to being in a state of relatively constant perspiration. Indeed the ability to appear completely indifferent to this is one of the great bond-builders among longtime Asia operators. Being at one with your own sweatiness can be a source of profound comfort. But even by my standards, the current climate was supplying new sensations of saturation. Nevertheless, even allowing for the tiring effect of this, there was surprisingly little chatter among our group. I would have thought that some might have emerged by now. After all we knew very little about one other. Not that I really wanted to know much more about any of them, less still engage in discussion, but there was nothing else to do. The vast, endless rainforest held nothing of interest. I asked Paul Hippie what he did for a living, adding, "Before you came here."

He looked at me as we walked and seemed unwilling to answer. Training had taught him not to talk. Then, "Absolutely nothing. Nothing compares to what I'm doing now."

Were you rich or poor? I asked.

"Rich," he delivered.

How rich? Very rich?

"No. Just rich. Rich enough not to ever worry about bills. No need to cook for myself. That rich."

Not so rich, I decided. Really rich people never think of cooking as a chore. How many cars did he have?

"One."

What did his mother and father do for a living?

He never answered and I was left to look at the scenery.

Overall I was still feeling much more relaxed about everything, having recovered the leisure bag and in particular the flask. As I have already noted, the flask of 110-proof vodka was an emergency provision that it had never been necessary to use. It is enough to know that, at any time, in any public or private place – shopping mall escalator or primary school, butcher's shop or stable – one has about oneself sufficient alcohol to get completely drunk with a minimum of fuss. It is one of the few blessings of modern life that intoxication is seldom out of reach, given a clutch of credit cards, a British passport and a determined attitude. The new-found relevance of the flask was not in its contents; it was in the vindication that I had been right to have it all along. Vindication is the greatest of feelings. Seek it out. Fondling the flask now as it nestled inside the bag was almost enough to turn me all Roman Catholic. This was my artifact. All things told, I was in a much better frame of mind. The only real dilemma to be faced was whether or not to have some or all of the vodka. But then something disturbing happened.

From the front of the column we became aware of a rising voice. And although we were hush before, we became even husher. Patrick Baker, accompanying Roger, was arguing with him. Roger's replies were, undoubtedly, calm, reasoned, quiet. The baker's questions or accusations were not.

"Piece of stuff and nonsense this. Trying to save the bloody world by kidnapping us, me . . . a baker!

"I'm a baker for God's sake . . . a baker!" he spluttered.

"This does seem rather a bit of gesture politics, at best."

It was the architect, adding to the stew. Normally I would not have said a thing myself. It is generally best to say nothing. Volunteering an opinion is a desperately silly thing to do. Perhaps the slightly unusual situation impaired my judgment. Because in response to the architect's mild observation, I found myself saying, "Quite right."

To which, ever so quietly, came Elizabeth's sly, university-graduate response, replete with supreme smugness: "What do you know about this? You're just a salesman."

Ouch. This was of course true. I was just a salesman. Just one of the small people in their Large-Scale World. I could remember in my youth how ashamed I had been of my profession. This was in the days before I realized that the type of job you do to get your money is of no consequence whatsoever. Friends of the period, long gone now, thankfully, would churn over the various policy aspects they were working on in this bank or that civil service or at such and such a level. Gradually from this period an awareness arose on my part. People had to make what I sold. Other people depended upon me to make sales happen. Without my sales the cupboard of many would be bare. And not just the cupboard; the bookshelf, the wardrobe, the car boot, the social diary. The four great containers of modern life. All would be empty without my efforts and those of thousands of sales professionals around the world. Christmas would not take place – who would pay for the children's presents? Where would family holidays come from? I and others like me were the cement of contemporary society. In US Army parlance, we were the grunts – the foot soldiers of capitalism. We had all fought our own Dunkirks; we had all at some point supported wounded colleagues without a second thought for individual monthly targets.

I am too modest to claim any special honors for myself. Indeed I was not even sure if my machines were entirely British-made and thus stoking purely British furnaces. I had, though, seen and met many persons who clearly carried the strain of supporting whole communities in their combination-lock briefcases. I would not let this jungle idealist stain their character without challenge. I blinked vociferously and cleared my throat. Then cleared it again.

"Yes, I am a salesman and salesmen have rights, too. My rights come from the same place yours come from, Elizabeth."

People who dislike you are always tremendously irritated when you address them politely and use their first name. Elizabeth was indeed momentarily taken aback, though her face quickly snapped back into the disgusted snarl which she seemed to have worked on especially for me. This brief exchange silenced the group for a moment. But Patrick Architect had been ignited and was not about to let things drop.

"How exactly do you intend to convince the world that you mean business?"

"How do you mean, Patrick?" Roger replied, playing dumb very badly. To correctly play dumb you do not pretend you do not understand – you answer another question entirely. For example:

SALES DIRECTOR: Are you or are you not going to achieve the sales targets we set six months ago?

SALESMAN: Was it really six months ago? My, how time flies.

Wrong. Right:

SALESMAN: I think we're playing golf on Thursday.

The architect was unstoppable. "Well, Roger, if I was the outside world receiving your ultimatum, I would want proof that you did indeed have us in captivity. Then I would need to satisfy myself that you were the type of people ready and willing to murder us if your demands were not met. One without the other is meaningless. Is that clear enough?"

A fair summation of hostage logic, I felt. Roger paused, halting the column.

"It may be necessary to convince the relevant people that one or two of you have been captured and dealt with. To this end we may have to shave off a bit of your hair or something. Nothing serious."

Patrick Architect did not respond and we moved off again. If he or any of the others thought that a single lock of hair was going to achieve anything they did not say so. I was far from convinced. Kidnappers need to demonstrate their willingness to extinguish life at a moment's notice; they need to show how cruel they are. The severing of a quiff of hair could never be viewed as a demonstration of terrible cruelty. Unless your name was Bill Haley. And if it had been, none of us would have been there.

At night we came to rest with relief. There was a solid urgency to our camp-setting which made it clear that the day was no longer wanted. We Patricks were required to help only with the defining of the clearing itself. The setting of tents, cooking implements and so forth was the work of the captors and was well rehearsed. The whole process took less than thirty minutes. I found my eyes on the figure of Elizabeth. She worked with a diligence bordering on devotion. Her young and fanciful dreams had forced her on a journey of danger. What a bold and beautiful woman she was. Despite our earlier exchange in the rainforest I felt no anger, as I knew that she was as much a captive of this whole affair as me. People who have a certain high level of beauty can only have wholly innocent motives. Experience had taught me this. Or else they are prostitutes.

Goodnights were exchanged and the light linen sheets that covered us were a silent draping of the day gone by. All was hush. I sensed that everyone was most soundly asleep. I alone lay quietly, eyes open still, my thoughts ravished with the taste of bourbons, gins and tequilas until I could feel the water running from my teeth. I lay on top of the flask, trying desperately to smother its call. It would not do to drink it now. Sleep came slowly and the fervent fire in my belly made its arrival harrowing, unwelcome, impertinent.

8. THE DUKE OF SUNG

Someone was talking. It was still completely dark. The kidnappers were in conference. I had come to abruptly and quickly tuned in, trying to pick up whatever tidbits I could. Roger was lecturing on someone called the Duke of Sung. The hushed tones did not make listening easy, added to the fact that I dared not move a muscle lest I alert them. The Duke of Sung seemed to be a leader or military figure of some sort. Elizabeth interrupted, to general approval, with a statement about the anachronistic concept of royalty. Roger explained that the Duke was Chinese, which seemed to satisfy the policy of accepting all sorts of Oriental tat as in some ways valuable whereas anything of Western origin was inherently worthless. The gist of the story seemed to be that this Chinese general refused to act without honor and was subsequently defeated, along with his people, by less scrupulous opponents. There was no doubt what Roger said next, because he raised his voice, firmed it up.

"Do we all understand? Do we all understand why the Duke of Sung failed?"

I could picture them all nodding like donkeys. Roger was happy.

"Good."

With slow, practiced moves the kidnappers ungrouped and stealthily repositioned themselves. After a moment all was quiet. Soon, merciless sleep dragged me back under.

I like watching other people waking up. I can't imagine anyone who wouldn't. The trees obscured the sunrise almost completely but this did not stop the group's vague outline being described in a tender orange light. I had woken close to the first streak of day and slowly taken in the scene around me. The same seven bodies. Watching other people wake is such a pure, happy thing – a birth without the blood. The slight head turns, the body rolls, the hand dragged across the face. These thoughtless, uncontrived movements are truly beautiful in their innocence. I propped myself up on one elbow to get a better view. Only Roger was quite motionless. With steady, measured breathing he slept with the type of intensity one always envies. Not for him the fitful sleep of a doubt-swept mind. I was wondering when and in what order they would stir when the piercing bleep-bleep of a wristwatch broke the moment. I quickly sank back down into a sleeping position. There was no point in stirring properly before it was absolutely necessary. Besides which it was preferable for someone else to shoulder the burden of saying "Good morning" to everyone as they awoke. When you're the last to get up it's easy to act grumpy and be excused the dreary routine of greeting. I lay still trying to decide whose watch it was. It was Roger's. With a deft flick of his hand he silenced it. Turning, I saw that Elizabeth was in that midway point between sleep and stirring. Her beauty was more desperate than ever. Even lying here in the jungle, with the odd hair matted to her forehead and in need of a good wipe across the nose and mouth, there could be no doubt that she was a devilishly attractive woman. At the side of her eyes were the slightest of wrinkles, the early-morning kind that are so attractive in the opposite sex. The gentle movements of her face accentuated these lines wonderfully. I was terrified that one of the others might get up now and force the issue, jolting Elizabeth into uninspired animation before her time. I cursed silently each stirring of the jungle, each insect blip, each bird tweet. Elizabeth's right arm was now joining in. It moved to her forehead and swept softly upward. A single hair bounced back and placed itself over her left eye, lying gently across the bridge of her nose. Her hand returned to sweep again but missed, forcing her to shake her head slightly in an effort to move the tickling hair. I reached out and moved it for her. She awoke instantly, even before my hand had completed its upward journey. I smiled and she slapped me viciously across the cheek. The noise woke everyone and we plummeted without mercy into cacophony.

Elizabeth slapped me several more times before she was restrained by the well-rested Roger. There was no point in trying to explain. I smiled broadly, a tactic learned in China. Whenever you have done something quite wrong, even very wrong, it's as well just to smile when found out. Looking sheepish doesn't achieve much whereas a broad grin can really upset people.

Beatings aside, mornings are the worst times to catch me. Business life is crammed to bursting with these jolly types who seem to feel that behaving like some cheery chat show host first thing in the morning is part of their job description. If you want to find the effective salesman at any hotel buffet breakfast, look for the one who is conserving his bonhomie.

So I sat quietly munching my muesli while departure preparations were made. The other Patricks talked among themselves; the usual tedium of family, job, sports interests. They indicated with the odd casting of eyes and shifting of seating positions that I should join them. Such, in effect, flirtatious behavior is so degrading. I was once prevailed upon by a group of media sales executives – a chance encounter in the bar – to join them at dinner. Fearing a week-long valley of such evenings to ride through, I took a glass of wine and then collapsed face down in the consommé. Thereafter they kept their distance.

Had I not been keeping myself to myself, I would not have been watching our kidnappers quite so closely. I would not have noticed the intense passion with which they each went about their business. There is something about the countenance of those happily engaged in a menial task that guards against interference. The intent on their faces and the firm movement of the hands form a self-contained, ignorant beauty, a sight as calming as that of newborn gazelles at play in the Serengeti dusk. I caught Sally Hippie's eyes as she looked up momentarily, searching for some bag or other. Self-consciously she adjusted her top, then resumed her task. And there could be no doubt of the reason behind her guilty pause. Nestling beneath her armpit was the unmistakable outline of a revolver. A quick scan around her colleagues was sufficient to confirm suspicions. There seemed now little doubt to me that something substantially more than a quiff of hair was going to be required of us Patricks. The architect's observations about the need to communicate intent, coupled with Roger's own earlier thoughts on the need to shock, pointed firmly in the direction of a death. Moreover, the gist of the Duke of Sung pep talk was equally clear – he was preparing them for some questionable action. Furthermore, when examining Paul Hippie, our eyes also met. But, unlike Sally, he did not seem guilty. Rather he had about him a happy, distant look. And then I recognized the smile. It was precisely the same smile I had seen on a television program about peasant revolutionaries, when the old mayor was ostentatiously refused service in the village shop. Paul's was the smile of the assistant stacking the shelves at the time. In that instant it all came together – I knew the game. Patrick Robertson was going to die – all of us. There was no doubt what had to be done. With an easy casualness I reached for the vodka.

Alcohol is not the answer to all our problems. But if one removes from one's life those problems that cannot be solved with alcohol, the path is clear. Families are a particular nuisance. Get rid of them as soon as possible. With them go all the other responsibilities which require sobriety: pets, in-laws, other parents, Sunday mornings. The principal improvement drink brings is in the area of decision-making. Indeed, it is difficult to maintain a consistent level of rashness without alcohol. Furthermore, it is not simply in terms of direction that alcohol helps in decision-making. There are plenty of lateral-thinking schemes and so forth which could supply equally obtuse options. It is, however, only alcohol that provides the energy and verve required to power the action immediately once a decision is made. Thus, in one dramatic surge, alcohol can fire you, unaware and unprepared, into total commitment. It is the very stuff of deliverance.

At this stage I did not need to use any of the vodka. Experience taught me that the intimation of consumption is sufficient to kick-start the mind. One truth shone like a beacon. A salesman learns early on that, despite operating under the same name, with the same ostensible objectives, more ill can come through sharing information and plans with your workmates than with the supposed opposition. True salesman do not hunt in packs. When the time came for whatever was required, I would once more be on my own. That thought in itself was sufficient inspiration for any action that would be required.

Over my muesli, a basic list of requirements was formed. I would need food, water and the maps. Most important, I would need to create an opportunity.

The deliberate sacrifice of one's colleagues is not something that should be an ordinary part of your agenda. It is not something to be proud of. On only one previous occasion had I acted in such a fashion. Early on in my career I had been sent out to secure a major turning-screw foundry deal in Malaysia. I was not as yet on the Asia circuit. This sudden release from the strictures of both family and company disciplines provoked a massive binge. At that point I had not yet achieved the ability to masquerade as diligent, responsible and effective while either marginally sober or suicidally hung over. Thing went badly. After three days I knew that the deal was lost. Nevertheless a positive stream of communication with HQ was maintained, with increasingly fictional content. Finally the crunch came. Instinctively I requested the urgent dispatch of one of my colleagues to assist in the closing stages. Such assistance is quite commonplace on larger deals, particularly when one is a relative beginner. Tom Huntly had joined Mackenzie Industries at the same time as me. We had trained together, even gone drinking of an evening. Tom arrived in a state of some excitement, this being his first trip abroad also. I took him through some made-up documents before getting him absolutely drunk and arranging for several hookers to visit his room in an all-night relay session. Next morning I, regrettably, had food poisoning and was unable to accompany the much-depleted Tom to the climactic meeting. I can still imagine his trembling body taking its final blow as, upon opening his briefcase with relative confidence, he found it filled with nothing but empty writing pads. I did not escape entirely from the repercussions, but it was Tom who got the heave-ho. People who are that easily set up aren't worth having in your company anyway. So it would be with the other Patrick Robertsons. They would be my springboard back to freedom and the life I knew and missed so much.

The role of misinformation would be crucial. There are a couple of paths to avoid in successfully conveying misinformation. For example:

CUSTOMER: Are you sure this model will satisfy my requirements?

SALESMAN: Needs are never static. Based on our discussion, and your plans, I see no reason to think that this machine will not meet, and indeed exceed, your requirements.

Unfortunately there are a significant number of customers who are not complete fools and won't permit such brazen skullduggery. This is the correct pattern:

CUSTOMER: How sure can I be that this machine, despite being apparently less well equipped than that of your competitors, has the required flexibility for my plans?

SALESMAN: Completely.

End of story. There is a time and place for the truth, and the conclusion of a sales pitch is not it. Remember that all sales are merely the beginning of a relationship. The important thing is to get the relationship started. Save the truth for those moments in life when it is absolutely fitting, such as when explaining to your wife that the company of whores is both preferable and, in the long term, cheaper.

I started with the architect, waiting until everyone's attention was elsewhere.

"I think they're going to kill us and I think they're going to do it soon."

He nodded sanguinely. Occasionally one can score a direct hit, such as this, when one's own suggestion glides easily into a tailor-made opening. I placed my hand on his lower arm, the ultimate man-to-man action for demonstrating honesty.

"Patrick, something will happen on the trail today. When it does, do not hesitate. All Patricks must run off to the immediate left. I will secure the maps and supplies. If need be I am quite ready to make the ultimate sacrifice. We cannot let this go on."

I gripped his arm tightly and stared off into the middle distance, where all valor is to be found. Releasing him, and allowing for a safe amount of time, I moved on to Patrick Computer. He received the same instructions. I ended at Patrick Baker. We chatted amiably about the weather, spending sufficient time so as to convince the other Patricks that the same procedure was being followed. I also emptied one of his two water bottles when no one else was looking, replacing the contents with a good measure of vodka. Redemption can often involve truly horrendous sacrifices.

9. REAFFIRMATION

The heat poured ever on. Our bodies had been drenched in sweat from the very first. Roger's pervasive air of determined virtue seemed to inure the kidnappers to such distraction. I reflected ruefully on the fact that the combined effect of a general lack of alcohol, a diet of nutritional food and a regime of constant exercise would have a beneficial effect on my physical health. What use is that to me? Just as a slug needs the cool comfort of the belly of a boulder, so I require the shelter of an anonymous hotel bar. It is in the avoidance of life that one is best placed to enjoy it.

Roger had explained at length that we must conserve our water supplies. He had also explained that, if necessary, it was possible to collect water from the morning dew so that we need have no absolute fears of dying of thirst. Furthermore, additional stores lay waiting at our destination. Nevertheless the warning was sufficient and despite the heat everyone was being frugal with the water. I watched and waited.

We stopped for a mid-morning break. Everyone reached for their water bottles. With every muscle tense I watched the baker take a mouthful. Nothing; the wrong bottle. Still I felt happier. All knowledge is power; the other bottle would be the one for sure. Over the course of the morning I watched as, bit by bit, the baker drained the first. At lunch, a tasteless assortment of stodgy veggie-bars, he finished it completely.

It seemed about one hour after we sent off again that I saw Patrick Baker searching round his waist for the other bottle. I braced myself for action. Finally he found it, undid the stopper and took a long draught. For anyone who has not tried neat vodka, the first time always delivers an exceptional kick. All the more so when the spirit is 110 proof.

A quick word on the proofing system. It is quite common to hear people in bars talking loudly about how drunk they were or how much some acquaintance can hold and so forth. Apart from the fact that talking about heavy drinking is the stuff of real bores, it is often the case that reference is made to 100 percent proof this or that. This is, of course, utter nonsense. The percentage score one sees on the side of a bottle of alcohol refers to the percentage of the bottle's contents that are alcohol. Thus one liter of wine contains, typically, 135cl of alcohol, i.e., is 13.5 percent alcohol. This is not the same as "proof." "Proof" refers to an old system for measuring alcoholic strength. Avoid using it unless you know what you're doing. Stick to the percentages.

Swallowing exceptionally strong, neat spirits is a trial magnified one hundredfold when one is not expecting it. The baker imploded on the spot, doubling over in violent seizures. He wanted to cry out but was unable to as the raw fire of the vodka scraped his stomach. Roger immediately dropped his packs and was on his knees beside him. I shouted, "Patrick!" As Paul Hippie surged past me to lend further assistance I extended a foot, sending him sprawling across the ground. The two remaining Patricks turned and from my face understood that now was the time. Immediately they bounded off to the left. I raced forward, kneed the shocked Roger in the face, grabbed his packs and fled with all my might into the thick jungle to the right. Behind me, the distressed cries and shouts of the group fuelled my flight to safety.

I did not stop running for what seemed like half an hour, during which time I dodged this way and that, shaping what I hoped to be a crooked, difficult route for anyone to follow. Almost too soon the distant calls of "Patrick! Come back!" faded entirely. At one point I thought I heard several shots. Lungs bursting, I collapsed behind a large, fruity bush and curled myself up, coughing, wheezing, rejoicing, laughing, living. In that moment I knew the exquisite beauty of finding that which I did not know had been lost. I was the Patrick Robertson again.

I woke at the first intrusions of dusk, still feeling exhausted. There was a backpack to my left, which I hastily opened. Assorted food packages, cutlery, water purification tablets, a couple of sleeping slips, two T-shirts, a pencil, two side-strapped water canisters, two PVC sheets. A fair booty. In the other pack, more food packets and more water tablets. And the maps. Fifteen in all; large, mesmerizing studies in green, with the blue scratches of hidden waters. All of them appeared to be the work of Bartholomew's of Edinburgh from sometime in the Fifties.

There is about maps the greatest sense of absolute information combined with minimal knowledge. They only begin to have real meaning when brought into contact with the here and now. When traveling it was a favorite pastime of mine to turn to the map section at the back of the in-flight magazine and, taking from my pocket a packet of colored dot stickers, affix them to the sites of major airline crashes or in-flight disasters. This action would inevitably raise the interest of the neighboring chump who, egged on by his free booze, would make inquiry and then listen with some degree of, at worst bemusement, at best sheer terror, as the purpose was explained. By raising one's voice appropriately it was usually possible to ensnare most of the immediately surrounding rows, too. Without maps this exercise would have been quite impossible.

Becoming fully conscious, my fear of being found by Roger and his gang increased. Although, looking anxiously around me, nothing seemed to indicate imminent recapture, I decided that it would be prudent to push as far on as possible before nightfall. I rummaged round in the bag for a quick biscuit. There was no clue as to which direction should be taken, although I felt that the kidnappers had been left somewhere over my right shoulder. I stood up, closed my eyes and listened tightly. Just the jungle – a pervasive wall of insects.

I lugged the backpack on and headed off on a bearing that I hoped would take me far, far away from the group. After what could not have been more than twenty minutes I realized that I was semi-running; certainly moving very fast for me, continually glancing over one of my shoulders, lest someone be approaching. But as night descended I began to feel more confident that I was on solid solitary ground. Underneath a deep blue sky I wrapped myself up in sheeting, alone and, for what had been achieved that day, content.

The next morning I had been walking for three or four hours when I began to have doubts about my route. Despite having Roger's compass I had no idea how to determine correct position or direction. However, without maps my erstwhile captors would be increasingly occupied with their own survival; my recapture would be a distinctly secondary issue. As such, the seizure of the maps was a tactical success. I myself can no more read one than snare a baboon. Looking back I could barely make out the trail by which I had traveled. The thought of the others scrambling around all over the place amused me greatly.

I became conscious that being in any way hunted fills one with a sense of awareness quite lacking in normal life. Compared to the tired habits of the modern world that we so laughingly call hobbies, an innovative Random Deathhunt – licensed by the authorities to a suitably qualified operator (ex-Prison Service?) – would surely liven up many lives. The game could be conducted on a weekly basis. Indeed, it could be the corollary of those national and state lotteries that have popped up all over. These things are all give and no take and would surely benefit from a bit of rebalancing.

Regardless of misgiving about direction, there was no option other than to carry on. Simply because one fears that one is getting nowhere is no reason to stop. For most of a salesman's life the overwhelming feeling is of "getting nowhere." The only option is to keep going. Consider the situation of the salesman on a particularly tough call.

CUSTOMER: I have no interest in what you're selling.

SALESMAN: I can understand your reticence, but if you look at all the facts...

CUSTOMER: Listen to me – Not now. Not ever. Now – I'm very busy. So if you'll excuse me.

SALESMAN: I'll call back at some other time.

CUSTOMER: Don't bother.

The correct action for the salesman following the above encounter is simple – forget it. Make a note in your own diary to call again in one month. Then on to the next customer. Do not spend one second thinking about the conversation. Customers overestimate how heavily such conversations hang on a salesman. In truth it is the customer who is the tedious intrusion, like stepping on chewing gum. Get rid of it and move on. Keep going regardless.

I keep going. Even when there was at most half an hour or so before absolute dark, I resolved to make the most of it, forcing myself firmly through the trees. Somewhere a hotel bar was waiting. I would have hummed something, perhaps even sung, had the fear of my pursuers not been so strong. Moreover, where tunes were concerned, my mind was rather blank. This is not altogether surprising. Very little of what passes for contemporary popular music is either interesting or memorable. Modern songs, for example, seldom feature the words "My dear." How much better if they did. A happy achievement indeed. Then they would truly be fit for public consumption – not the splatter of ironic commentary that we have to digest with even the simplest foot-tapping melody. No, the songs of today are not of the type that could play across the lips while riding a horse on the way to market, or gazing with a loved one fondly over the city at sunrise. We are in desperate need of yearning yet hopeful songs centered on the emotions of ordinary people. Certainly nothing came to mind as I made my way with increasing adeptness from tree to tree. Nimbleness, I thought, even without a tune, is nice.

Sitting at camp that night, I realized that almost twice as much ground must have been covered as might have been with the group. Even setting up had been quicker. I had stamped around on my own, making a nice, flat area, then easily got the little camping stove going, boiling up an instant veggie-steak with potatoes and beans. The sun had set almost without me noticing, and I was marvelously alone under the jungle canopy. I had prepared my bed when there had been a little light left and I now crawled under the sheet. As best as possible I made a sealed unit to sleep in. I curled up inside it and let the cover close above me.

10. THE WANDERING DUE

There is no real weather in the rainforest. The air presses down and in on you tightly. Every day is like the last. I had been on the move for about seven days when this struck me. By now my eyes had adapted to the density of the foliage, just as one's eyes adapt to the dark. It was possible to pick out individual bushes more quickly. There was a completeness to the green but it was only being caused by a few plants. I remembered Roger wittering on about how there were over 250 species of tree in one hectare. I could only see four or five and even they were pretty similar.

  While at tree-top level there was an almost complete roof of indistinguishable green, I could now pick out the patterns on the ground, see the groupings of plants and trees. The largest clumps of ground vegetation were around fallen trees. The holes in the roof that resulted from the collapse of bigger trees allowed a flood of light into a highly concentrated area, creating islands with a great deal of care. They were just such places that would undoubtedly prove attractive hiding places for tigers and the like. There they would wait for less diligent business travelers than myself, for those who would stray too close, perhaps enchanted by the "house on the plain" appearance that these growth spots gave. In a flash their thoughtlessness would result in a swift paw from behind and a short struggle to a gory end.

On the tenth day I found the bodies. There were four. Two Patricks, architect and baker, and Paul and Sally Hippie. They appeared to have caught something, their faces spotty and bloated. I kept well back. There was no sign of anything worth salvaging; indeed it appeared that someone else had already done that, presumably Elizabeth, Roger and Patrick Computer.

That afternoon I found myself longing for the comforts of the job for the very first time. I pictured myself placing orders down the phone to my contacts in England, sending confirmatory faxes. The solid machinery of Mackenzie Industries would stir, grinding out the appropriate responses, shipping orders and engineers as required. My heart swelled to imagine those magnificent men and women, now giving television and radio interviews about me – "Colleagues of the missing man described him as clever and well dressed." They would explain who I was – a wily adventurer who had done much in difficult markets through difficult times to keep the sales coming in; how adeptly I had ensured that those would-be competitors were thwarted time and time again as they sought to encroach on our area; how moderate my expenses were, in general. For all these achievements and more I was being venerated in many tongues; perhaps even with subtitles.

I soldiered on. The small, dehydrated packets of food were providing sufficient, if not stimulating, nutrition. By now I was well into the water purification tablets. Roger seemed to have been carrying many weeks' supply of them. My hair was firmly matted to my head with a fast grip surpassed only by that which affixed my underpants to my buttocks. Having encountered no leeches whatsoever I had long discarded the gaiters; either the leeches were all on holiday or, more likely, Roger had simply invented them so as to increase his power over us. Strangely, I still had what remained of the vodka. It had acquired for me the aura of a talisman and I was loath to drink it. This was fortunate because two days later I was able to give some to Elizabeth before she died.

Roger and Elizabeth were slumped side by side over their packs about ten miles from where I found the others. Their hands were clasped tightly together. They had about them the presence of children asleep in the back seat of a family car. Warily I circled the bodies. There was no sign of disease or infection. When I bent down to inspect them further, Elizabeth opened her eyes and smiled. A hand moved forward, searching for some human contact. "Patrick," she breathed out through cracked, fragile lips. I took her delicate fingers in mine.

Death is something best avoided in life. Once, during a regional sales conference in Macau, one of my colleagues was fucked to death by a teenage Vietnamese lap dancer. I was in the neighboring room and was woken by her screams. Entering the room I found the girl sitting on the edge of the bed, my colleague slumped lifelessly over a pile of pillows. This was a happily married father of three with a good pension fully paid up. Immediately assessing the situation, I paid the girl to disappear, then dragged my colleague to the balcony, stripping him and dropping him eight floors into the swimming pool. I was hopeful that the case would be assessed as a midnight swim gone tragically wrong. As it was he lived for two days before ultimately succumbing to the extreme injuries sustained on impact with the bottom of the pool. The verdict was suicide and the pension was lost. It's best not to get involved with death.

"Patrick," Elizabeth whispered again. I nodded in acknowledgment.

"Patrick, we had no food – you took most of it."

"I know, Elizabeth, I know," I said comfortingly.

"And no water tablets – you had them all."

"I know, Elizabeth," I repeated softly with feeling.

She seemed to close down for a moment. When she resurfaced, her gaze was heavenwards. I joined her in consideration of that above.

"My life has been a complete failure," she burbled. "I am a failure."

This was not strictly true. Elizabeth was a loser, not a failure. Failures are, on the whole, interesting people. Failures have gambled and lost, battled and been defeated, been conned, swindled, have dived and bobbed before finally realizing that the world has not been made for them to succeed in. They end up as small-town barkeepers, second-hand (but not antiquarian) booksellers, self-employed business consultants. Cooking is one of the skills common to most failures. For conversation they have the inexhaustible arsenal of a life of strenuous activity thwarted by bureaucracy, public indifference or Other People. Driven by conviction, they have pursued the romantic idyll for many years, before dropping unrewarded, unrecognized, unwanted into anonymity. Losers, on the other hand, are just losers.

Elizabeth exhaled deeply. I sensed the end was near. I had arrived just in time. Quickly unscrewing the top of the vodka, I held it to her lips, then upended it so that a long stream of liquid burned its way down into her very soul. Her eyes shot open, she squealed briefly, then collapsed into my arms and breathed no more. I cannot think of a better way to go.

There was very little of worth to be had in Roger and Elizabeth's packs. It did indeed seem that I had taken most of the food with me when I fled. There were a couple of cleanish T-shirts and two more gas stove canisters – predictably unused – but little else I fancied. I laid both bodies flat on the ground, crossed their arms and left them to the jungle.

Later, preparing for sleep, I had a feeling of real accomplishment. I had acted positively at the end of a fellow human being's life. People could live more happily if they thought that when their final moment came it would be in good company. If they knew that it might be with someone like me.

I never did find Patrick Computer.

11. LOST AND FOUND

My memories of this period are haphazard. Although I had food, there was not a lot and a degree of rationing was required. Furthermore, the sustained diet of purified water was not to my liking and I experimented with unpurified water from various pools and streams that I found. As a result there was a fairly constant diarrhea. This general weakening of my constitution did not stop me continually moving. But it did affect my ability to count hours and days with any precision. Indeed, psychologically, I was far from my best. I was down to my last piece of clothing; a long, baggy cotton top featuring two cuddly, indeterminate animals standing in front of a castle. Six days after leaving Roger and Elizabeth my position was bleak. There was maybe four days' food left, three days' water tablets. Most worryingly, I had a beard. Feeling it there every day, growing, brooding, on my face was a menace totally unforeseen. I'd never had more than two days' growth before, let alone a full beard. The avoidance of a beard or a five o'clock shadow is one of the simplest ways to ensure a happy, unquestioned existence. In modern times the appearance of any form of facial hair is always considered "strange." At the Mackenzie Industries Sales Training School I made the point succinctly to the last class I was called to address; many a sales deal has been lost because, at the point of pen being put to paper, the customer has looked up and seen a tell-tale glimmer of growth on the salesman's chin.

Walking and walking, my mind swam with images, thoughts and sensations from the life I treasured so much. I could smell the crisp, purified bed linen – top sheet turned so invitingly back, tenderly layered with a comforting fawn blanket. The white bathrobe, monogrammed Kuala Lumpur Hilton or Singapore Inter-Continental, swathed me as I stepped onto the balcony. Behind, the belly of the mini-bar had been exposed, suckling me with warm, flavorsome intoxication. My shoes were outside the door for cleaning. A bottle of wine was on its way. This is the wonderful world of the true traveler. Now as far from me as the day I was born.

There was nothing else to be missed. A wave of petty incidents had no doubt occurred. There had been a currency crisis somewhere; a racing driver had died; one big company had gone belly-up; another had been taken over. A war had been found by some particular media group and was now being touted to its audience as the next Lebanon/Yugoslavia/Whatever. Significant discoveries had been made about some type of cancer. Some famous people had died. Strange babies had arrived. None of these things would affect me in any way. The constants in my life never changed. I have often dreamt of the day when champagne is discovered spouting fountain-like from the earth and is henceforth dispensed to the needy by the United Nations. That would make a difference.

I stopped for a cup of tea. There were, perhaps, ten teabags to go. There was no avoiding the fact that the last sands of grain were surely trickling out of my hourglass. Something had to be done. I had a duty to try. Just then I recalled reading of a lost camper who had signaled to the outside world by arranging sticks in an SOS message on the hillside so that his plight might be visible to any aerial search parties. The story must have been in an in-flight magazine. He had died nevertheless but everyone agreed he had been a clever chap to have thought of the sticks. His mother said that ingenuity ran in the family. I felt that I should do the same. Indeed, looking up I saw that the leafy ceiling was beginning to show gaps. Perhaps this was intended as some form of encouragement. All that was needed was a hole in the trees big enough for my message to be read from the sky. I finished my tea, packed up and set out to find one.

Now I was walking with purpose. Purpose makes all the difference. My purpose was watching for a hole in the trees. Consider the difference between a purposeful and a purposeless cold (i.e., without an appointment) sales call.

SALESMAN: Good morning, I'd like to see someone about something. Is there anyone around?

RECEPTIONIST: No.

Not surprising, either. Contrast that with the following:

SALESMAN: Good morning, I'm here to put the new master account with Mackenzie Industries in place. Is there a room I can get set up in, please?

RECEPTIONIST: Um . . . I think Room 7 is free.

SALESMAN: Thanks. I'll need a bit of time. Maybe you could let them know I'll be ready in about fifteen minutes.

Leave it to the receptionist to figure out who "them" is. The point is you were purposeful; you're inside, in position, primed and ready.

Watching for holes in the trees proved a tremendous strain on my neck. After several hours I could keep it upright no more and let it droop. Quite unconsciously, I took off the backpack and peeled the last T-shirt from my back, throwing the soggy rag into the bushes. Realizing what had occurred, I felt a terrible sadness. I remember thinking we come into this world naked and now I was preparing to leave it. Shouldering the backpack, now eerily light of contents, I continued on. Not looking up; completely without purpose.

I was looking straight ahead, sitting down, leaning against a tree. The empty backpack was beside me; my life behind me. Ahead was green, dense, lush, square. *Square.* There was something square directly ahead of me, jutting out of the undergrowth. I don't believe in illusions so there was no doubting what I could see. I pushed myself up and stumbled forwards towards what was clearly a man-made item. About twenty feet later I was standing next to a huge wicker hamper, as if abandoned on some picnic expedition. There was some writing and what looked like logos on the side of the basket, reading at right angles to the ground and partially obscured by foliage. I reached out and brushed the leaves aside, then stepped back, breathless at my discovery. For there on the side of the biggest picnic basket I had ever seen was the unmistakable large red M and large blue I of Mackenzie Industries. They had found me. I was saved.

12. JUST DESERTS

Mackenzie Industries. I kissed it again, my arms embracing the fulsome wicker. It did not feel like wicker though, – it felt like plastic. Stepping back allowed me to focus on some bold black letters above assorted company logos; the wording was TRANS-ASIA BALLOON CHALLENGE. I walked round the basket. It was a hollow box. Assorted equipment, food and clothing were spilled out on the ground, dribbled from its mouth. A number of colored ropes snaked off into the bushes. There was a body. It lay slightly crumpled about two lengths from the upturned basket as if it had been coarsely spat out. A young man in a bright blue jumpsuit. A thin trail of blood ran from his crown and into a light red puddle in which a pair of sunglasses sat. He could not have been more than twenty-five years old. His face, while quite lifeless, showed none of the maggots or flies that I had been dreading. Clearly he had not been here long. The jumpsuit was covered with the names of various sponsoring companies, including my own. On the left breast was a name: Anthony Hislop was about four inches shorter than me and the jumpsuit did not fit perfectly. Still, it was almost entirely clean and made of some breathable fabric. I liked it. A new set of clothes brings out the best in anybody, whatever the circumstances. Tragically there was no mirror to hand.

The balloon basket did prove to be a hamper of sorts. The uppermost clasp-locked panniers inside the basket held plenty of food provisions: high-protein cereal bars, low-fat milk, shrink-wrapped preserved fruits, lots of chocolate. Strangely, there did not appear to be any alcohol. Not much of a journey, I thought. The idea of floating through the clouds in the company of a stiff vodka with several more glowing deep inside was quite exciting. So many potentially great times are ruined for want of a burst of alcohol. I recalled a taxi drive through Seoul with me standing in the passenger seat, my head sticking out of the sunroof. Had I not been outrageously drunk at the time, with a bottle of Dewar's whisky in either hand, it is most unlikely that I would have found this experience quite so exhilarating.

I must have been in a worse state than I thought. After gorging on several chocolate bars I collapsed into a deep sleep. Waking several hours later, I felt so much better. Refreshed enough to scrape out a slight hollow into which I rolled the body. Mackenzie Industries would surely appreciate the gesture.

Tucked into a side pocket of the basket was a plastic folder, stuffed with various printed memorabilia, a logbook, and a diary. Anthony Hislop's home town was Accrington, Ohio. The *Accrington Observer* had fine words for Anthony under the headline "ACCRINGTON BOY TO CROSS ASIA IN BALLOON." He had been top of his class at Benjamin Franklin High School before studying Business at Ohio State University, where he had discovered ballooning. He then joined the family grain business, becoming Finance Manager after one year. Such blatant nepotism makes my blood boil. One of the badges on his jumpsuit read "Hislop Holdings." He had been preparing for the Trans-Asia race for almost two years. A picture showed him in his jumpsuit with his mother and father standing in front of Hislop Holdings. They all looked feverishly happy, although Mrs. Hislop wondered how she would manage when Anthony was away. The article noted proudly that sponsorship had been secured from a number of international as well as national and local companies. Yet Mackenzie Industries were not mentioned by name and this annoyed me. We work hard at our business. As such, when we sponsor anything it is surely reasonable to expect the recipients to ensure as much publicity as possible. Perhaps this lack of sponsor acknowledgment was the underlying cause of Anthony's downfall. The invisible hand of capitalism is a strange and mighty force.

The rules of the Trans-Asia Balloon Challenge were clear. No use of transportation other than by balloon was permitted. No altimeters or anemometers or satellite navigation devices. No radios. No support teams were allowed to trail or precede the participants. It was the individual pilots alone who were responsible for all planning operations. It was they who decided where and when to set down. Timed to coincide with the late-autumn winds that sweep across the eastern globe, it had been anticipated that all pilots had a good to reasonable chance of skipping across the Asian continent, from takeoff in Central Japan to crossing the finishing line of 57 degrees latitude east – whatever that meant. Somewhere over Iran was, apparently, likely. Unprecedented international cooperation had been assured and sixty-five competitors from around the world had set off. An article clipped from *Time* magazine confirmed the status of the race. This was the toughest test in modern ballooning, with an ethos harking back to the fundamental challenges of the sport. Big deal. All I knew was that this balloon would be my ticket out of the jungle.

13. NO OTHER PEOPLE

How did this thing work? How did you start it? Was it broken? I considered the two journals. The logbook, stuffed with precise text, numbers, and measurements, looked the more likely to yield answers. The diary was some sort of soulful description of travel, with phrases like "My friend the balloon lifts my youthful body towards the heavens." I wedged it firmly under the right arm of the body of Anthony Hislop that he might carry it to the afterlife.

Anthony, the logbook's last entry indicated, had landed out of fear. His reading of the clouds ahead had indicated a massive storm. Furthermore, it continued, he had felt like a walk on solid ground anyway. I understood. Often when driving to a difficult meeting in my early days on the road back in Britain, I had pulled off for a drink or two. When young the avoidance of confrontation is the norm.

Following this, the logbook had only two further scrawled phrases – "Plain ahead," "Wind speed: Severe" – after which nothing. Clearly Anthony had got something terribly wrong. Nevertheless the implicit message from all of this was electrifying. If he was coming down alone, he knew he could get airborne alone. The need now was to find out how.

Salesmen find solutions. The first stage is to identify available resources. The best resources are, of course, Other People. Other People are the crash test dummies of effective business management. They do not help themselves by being forever keen to "get the job done," even if it's not their job. Their secret is simple – make your goal their goal. For example, you have just been informed of your forthcoming appointment as Sales Manager (Germany).

SALESMAN:(*Nonchalantly*) Have you heard the news about the board meeting?

DISPATCH MANAGER: No.

SALESMAN: Don't breathe a word of this but Mandy in Commercial said there's a major efficiency review planned. Apparently a lot of German customers are seriously unhappy with our performance on deliveries. Not that I care, like.

DISPATCH MANAGER: Gosh! Thanks.

The Dispatch Manager does not yet know about your move. The immediate increase in German customer satisfaction, as deliveries arrive on-time and error-free, will be put down to you. Warehouse people such as Dispatch Managers, are, quite rightly, never credited with anything.

Indeed, in many respects Other People are the only resource that matters. Computers, software, offices, money – the commonplace sandbags of siege-mentality management – are simply *things.* They in themselves won't do anything for you.

Regrettably the one Other Person who might have been employed in my cause lay dead. Therefore I was reduced to seeing what things I had.

The balloon sack itself, hanging loose from the trees like an empty breast, seemed in good condition. A side panel indicated that it was made from IMPERVION. None of the ropes or cables attaching it to the basket were broken. In between the sack and the basket, at the peak of a stainless-steel pyramidal structure pointing away from the basket, was a large gas-ring object: a burner for the hot air. Strapped underneath the basket were four silver tanks, which were in turn linked to the burner. A giant gas cooker.

I climbed into the overturned basket and began working through all of the compartments. Beneath the food was clothing: plenty of woolens, fleece and thermal insulation, all painstakingly rolled and stuffed into the precious space. Pushing my fingers into the tight, comforting gap between garments I recognized the careful composition of a studied piece of packing. In so doing, one of the golden rules of travel hit me on the chin: if carrying something fragile, such as anything jade or glass, make sure it is cushioned all around – clothing and/or towels are ideal. My hand delved deeper. There it was: hard, round – a bottle of something, wrapped in paper. With one almighty heave I pulled it out, sending clothes flying. Sitting against the wall of the basket I ripped off the white crepe paper. Golden Ohio Original Bourbone, a one-liter bottle. The "e" on the end of "Bourbon" was not a mark of quality. Everything I knew about alcohol told me that this would be strong, unrefined, and unpleasant. Without further thought I clawed the top off and fired a charge down, searing my throat with the spirit's natural fury. No doubt Anthony had envisaged a quiet, reflective glass of hometown bourbon on completion of the race. Quiet, reflective glasses of anything are a waste of time. In the silent glory of the moment it was impossible to tell whether the tears gliding down my cheeks were from the pain of the spirit or the elation of discovery.

I came to several hours later, having consumed only one quarter of the bottle. A further rummage produced some aspirin, which I choked down, followed by several nutritional fruit bars. Crawling out of the basket I banged my head on something – a control panel. Standing outside, I saw that the overall picture would be better if the basket were right ways up. With enormous effort I tipped it on to its bottom, then scrambled back in. The control panel was basic – an on/off button, next to a fuel gauge reading midway between "Empty" and "Full," next to a knob marked "Power" which could be set at "Ignition," then anywhere between 1 and 10. Under a flip-up transparent panel was a red switch reading "Inflate On" with a further switch marked "Flame." In one corner of the basket were two gauges – one for water, one for oxygen. These were the tools of escape.

Gingerly, I touched the "Inflate On" switch. It is not often one gets to touch things gingerly. Women in particular do not like gingerness; they like firmness. Deal with any woman on a "ginger" basis and they can really go off you. Always be firm. For example:

MAN: Would you care for dessert?

WOMAN: Perhaps. I'm not sure. Maybe I'll just go home.

See how quickly the woman became disenchanted when the decision was not made for her.

Contrast that with the following:

MAN: Right, main course over. Time for dessert.

WOMAN: God, I love you!

As with women, my ginger fingering produced nothing and I firmly moved the switch upwards. A sharp hum immediately surrounded me. Confused, I looked up and saw that the bottom half of the balloon was becoming taut. Fearing the worst, I pushed the "Inflate On" switch down and the balloon collapsed back into bagginess. I climbed up onto the wall of the basket.

Looking at the envelope of the balloon now it was possible to see veins running up and across the fabric, creating a lattice structure. It was this internal network which tightened once the "Inflate On" switch was thrown, shaping the rigid receptacle into which hot air could then be pumped. Hence, a solo takeoff was possible. I got out of the basket, excited and keen to be off, and hurriedly went through the items scattered over the ground. All of the food was to be taken, tawdry clothing discarded. The compartments at the bottom of the balloon could be explored in the air – I had no time to lose on such inventory just now.

Annoyingly, as I threw the last few packs of food into the basket it became quite clear that I would not be able to take off before sunset. An attempt in the dark was not attractive so there was no choice but to spend one more night in the rainforest. Mildly put out, I resolved nevertheless to sleep in the basket. Curling up inside, in a nest of new clothing, I took one small nip of the bourbon and collapsed into peaceful, hamster-like bliss.

14. PASSING THE BATON

Dawn came pronto. Resplendent in my new clothes I stepped out of the balloon and walked around it. A symptom of nervousness – nothing had changed. Anthony lay clasping his diary. Discarded clothes and food wrappers littered the area, like a horrible caravan site. For a moment I considered cutting off the colored ropes that fed out from each corner of the basket before deciding that they were probably there for some purpose or other. I climbed back in and had a fruit bar. Then another. More nervousness. Finally I gathered myself before the control panel and, this time with no hesitation, flicked the "Inflate On" switch. I was suddenly cocooned in the hum of the tightening balloon above me. There was a distant, muffled brushing as leafy branches were bent back by the expanding skin. Abruptly a strong bleep noise came from the panel. Dull rather than high-pitched or alarming, I realized it must indicate that the balloon was now primed for takeoff. Looking up I could see that the bottom of the sack was now a well-defined ball. I turned the "Power" knob to "Ignition," then flipped up the transparent cover and flicked the "Flame" switch. A sharp crack above my head made me duck. I looked up in time to catch the whoosh of the flame filling the gas ring. I turned "Power" to 5. The roar of the flame was immense, deafening; the air bending and folding as the torrent of heat surged upwards. I sat in one corner of the balloon, trembling, waiting. A long fifteen minutes passed before I felt the first stirrings of escape. The massive structure above me now blotted out the sky. It began to rock slightly back and forth, there was a violent lurch to the right and then we were rising. Not far and not fast, but rising nevertheless. Standing up to the edge, I watched the ground slowly recede. The rise was so gentle that it took me some time to realize it had stopped. Puzzled, I stood up to check. There could be no doubt. The balloon had stopped rising about fifty feet up. Yet the flame was still on; hot air was still being delivered into the envelope – what was wrong? I could see that most of the balloon had now cleared the trees – only me and the basket still dangled at bush level. Nothing appeared stuck. Agitated, I looked down. Looking up at me was the naked figure of Anthony Hislop, holding one of each of the balloon's red and blue ropes. As the balloon was hovering up, his head moving this way and that in an attempt to see who was in the basket.

"What happened? Who are you?" Anthony shouted.

My escape was now most precariously balanced. Goodness only knows what Anthony would do if he got me back on the ground. He would certainly want his clothes. But I needed to get back to my life! There was no choice to keep the balloon and continue on my way. Anthony's state of confusion would hopefully be my ally here.

"Anthony!" I called, trying to add a regal inflection to my voice.

"What? Who's that?" he asked, with some distress.

"Anthony. Listen to me. You are dead. Welcome to the afterlife."

I wanted to add, "Now let go of the ropes," but my salesman's training taught me I had to play it long-term.

"What?" he said after a brief pause.

"Anthony. I am the Spirit of the Life Past. I wear the clothes of your past existence." And I raised myself on tiptoe over the of the basket, holding my arms aloft in the pose of an angel seeking attention.

"Oh no, no no!" came the voice from below.

"You are now in Limbo, Anthony. You have been freed from your earthly bonds."

Silence, and then, in a tear-stained voice, "What happened to the balloon? I can't remember."

Looking down I could see Anthony on his haunches, though not yet letting go of the ropes.

"Anthony. The balloon crashed. You died instantly, but without pain."

He sat quite still.

"Anthony. Listen to me. You are dead. This is Limbo. Your naked soul must wander restlessly until your penance has been completed. Then you will be free to join the brighter spirits on the higher plain. But you must begin by accepting your place here." I waited. "Am I making the situation clear enough, Anthony?"

He looked up and I saw the glisten of moist cheeks.

"But I don't want to be dead," he wailed.

"Nobody does, at the time," I consoled him.

"My parents. I just wanted to make them proud. I love them so much," he burbled.

"Emma-Jane, my fiancée. She didn't even want me to do this. I love her so much."

It was time to get to the point.

"Anthony. You are now to begin your period in Limbo. You must demonstrate to all creation that you are prepared for the task ahead. Now – release the ropes."

Ever so slowly, he let go of the red rope. The balloon twitched slightly. But Anthony still held the blue rope and, watching him, his grip appeared to tighten. Now was not the time to be weak.

"Anthony, you must atone for your sins!" I commanded.

"But I don't know how to. I only wanted to be somebody. Accrington is such a small place and ballooning made me feel so good. Everybody used to come to the field . . ."

"Stop this immediately. What about your dirty past?"

He shuffled his feet slightly and, sensing a monetary advantage, I gathered my voice.

"You must atone for those sinful things in your past before you can join us above."

Crying overwhelmed him.

"Everyone has balloons in heaven, Anthony! But you must first pay for your deeds."

"How can I pay?" he shouted, falling to his knees.

"In the forest you will find the bodies of those who have failed to atone. Once you have buried them, then you will be clean enough to join us."

Abruptly, he let go of the rope. I threw out a couple of water bottles and a bag of foodstuffs, which landed near him. Anthony was oblivious to this, though, watching my ascent. I waved to him.

"We are waiting for you, Anthony," I shouted cheerfully.

He waved back and was still waving when the wind took the balloon and blew me away from the clearing and towards the brilliant sun.

15. UP AND DOWN

I woke semi-frozen. After takeoff I had had another quarter of the bottle of bourbon and could remember shouting at some clouds. Anthony's waving figure was but a memory. I could, of course, with a sharp increase in hot air, have taken off with Anthony dangling beneath me, but had he fallen that might have been murder. As it was he was in much the same position as I had been – not so much murder as jolly bad luck.

The exhilaration of ascent coupled with the alcohol must have shielded me from the sharp drop in temperature. I was now quite numb and ripped open a locker, desperate for warm clothes, settling on a T-shirt, a long-sleeve silk top, two woolen jumpers and a pair of thermal long johns. I stripped hastily to put these on, covering it all up with my new jumpsuit. Finally two pairs of gloves, three pairs of socks and a thick, woolly bobbly hat over an insulated balaclava. Then sun goggles. I would not normally have been seen dead in an outfit like this, but it is important to adjust one's wardrobe to fit the occasion. Even a desire or concern about having the right clothes yields positive results. For example:

HOTEL RECEPTIONIST: I'm sorry sir, but it is not permitted for guests to sleep on top of the bar.

SALESMAN: I seem to have lost my tie.

HOTEL RECEPTIONIST: Allow me to assist, sir.

A concern for one's dress demonstrates that one is of character and worthy of due respect. So imbued, anything is possible.

Before collapsing I had thankfully had the good mind to turn off the burner. Below me was a complete blanket of clouds, the type which always looks so inviting from an airplane window seat. I have often sat, nose pressed against the glass, large whisky in hand, considering the inviting duvet of whiteness below me.

Having established how to rise, it was appropriate to understand how to descend. Altering direction could not be in my power, I reasoned – there were no side jets or similar and the balloon must simply go where the wind took it. The lack of control over direction did not bother me. There were two ropes dangling down from the balloon; one yellow, one white. I tugged the yellow one and the balloon jerked downwards. I then tried the white and found the balloon turning clockwise around on the spot. Fat lot of good that was.

The logbook plotted Anthony's journey. From a start in Nagano, Japan, he had been blown over to mainland China, landing near Harbin and then drifting down the so-called Gold Coast, past Shanghai and right over Fuzhou, and then along to Guangzhou. From there he had set off for Thailand. This had taken about six weeks, what with waiting for prevailing winds and so forth. How marvelous, I thought. And even now Anthony was engaged in another magnificent adventure! I had a swig on the bourbon to his good health.

Over three days and nights I floated, standing to give the balloon a blast of hot air every hour or so, and for the rest of the time sat in a corner of the basket, eating food bars and the like, dropping the wrappers over the side. There was a reflective tarpaulin covering, which could be fastened over the top to conserve heat. At night I would give much bigger blasts of hot air, but only every two or three hours. My body is used to having bouts rather than lengths of sleep. The bourbon was all but gone. Only one large measure remained, which I sniffed at from time to time. Given the lack of control over direction there was no option other than to accept this aimless drift. The level of fuel in the tanks went down bit by bit. Yet each day, each hour, I felt the excitement of being that bit closer to where I belonged.

I had just completed going to the bathroom – a tiresome business involving plastic bags – on the fourth morning when I heard a noise – nothing clear, just "a noise." Immediately I checked the envelope. I heard it again. Looking up I could see no damage. I leaned over the basket and edged round the sides. Now the noise was more clearly defined – a drone of some sort, ever so distant. I shook my head slightly, cupping each ear alternately to check that this wasn't some internal malfunction caused by altitude. The noise was now a quiet, moody rumble. I turned towards the sun, squinting. Set against the dazzling horizon of light was the front-on silhouette of a Boeing 747, steadily closing on my position. If it did not hit me it would surely pass very close. I opened my mouth and nothing happened. I closed it again. Surely the pilot would have seen me. Watching closely, it was a relief to realize that the plane was not approaching nose-on and would not therefore impact directly. My next thought concerned being seen. This was all I needed. If my position was radioed in, then someone might come looking for me. But wait, no; if the balloon was spotted safe and flying, then any search parties currently investigating might be called off. It was therefore in my interest to be seen.

Now the plane was approaching at speed; a stark, growling predator. Leaning forward, I could just make out the distinctive markings of British Airways. My heart soared and I prepared myself to greet them. It was important that there should be no doubt that I was Anthony Hislop. I pulled the bobble hat further down, almost completely over my eyes, tugging up the collar on my jumper so that I covered my mouth. My face was now totally masked. Standing ready, I considered what would be happening on the airplane. The pilot and his crew, having ascertained that I was not a hazard, indeed having identified me from some schedule or other, were announcing at this point that on the left side of the plane passengers would be able to see a rare sight indeed: one of the participants in the Trans-Asia Balloon Challenge. This announcement would be the cause of much nudging with elbows. (There would of course be one or two non-English speaking passengers who would simply be alarmed). Children would be demanding access to windows and those seated next to windows would be feeling very proprietorial. Passengers would be scurrying back from the toilets and taking their positions. Maps were being consulted; approximate locations plotted, marked. Films were being eagerly loaded.

Then the gain was upon me. Not five hundred yards away were row after row of eager spectators. The crew in the cockpit were waving with the steady, reassuring tempo you would expect of experienced aviators. Predictably, the quality of the greeting on offer degenerated as one looked along the body of the aircraft. To the front, First Class affected a nonchalant, anonymous few fingers. Behind them Business Class were succinct and to the point; a strong, affirmative wave, a simple smile; a breezy, upbeat endorsement. Distressingly, after but a few rows of corporate reliability, Economy Class was the sad pandemonium one would have expected but hoped against. Miniature flash bulbs popped as faces, hands and bodies crammed and pushed against the windows for the full length of cabin. Towards the rear I was sure that actual fights were breaking out over viewing space. Economy children and babies were thrust up to fill entire panes, with invisible adults working their tiny hands into frenzied, puppet-like waving. The aircraft appeared to be angled slightly towards me as everyone moved over to the one side. To all of this I stood in quiet dignity: right hand raised to forehead, left hands straight own my side, sternly saluting the might of Western technology as it swiftly passed. The tail with the smallest of Union Jack emblems filled my heart and it was all I could do to hold the tears back. As the trail of flashbulbs disappeared into the blue yonder I held my position until certain I was out of sight. Then, relived and exhilarated, I knew I had earned my reward. I pulled the top from the bourbon and with one fleet hand-move mercilessly filled my mouth with the last of the spirit, forcing it down with glee.

I tossed the bottle over the side and sat down on the basket floor. The passing 747 had rekindled my spirits. I felt much more positive. Yet the need for control was also more apparent; I needed to feel more strongly that I was going somewhere.

I consulted Anthony's logbook. The last stated position was simply "North Thailand," followed by a string of meaningless numbers; Anthony's last reckoning point, anyway. I pulled myself up and looked over the sides. I had no information; no reference points of any sort. If I was able to see the ground, this would at least be a beginning. I reached up and pulled the yellow rope firmly. The balloon shuddered slightly and then, almost imperceptibly at first, began to sink towards the clouds. Where would I emerge? For all I knew I might have flown straight out over the Indian Ocean or north into Tibet. Nevertheless the 747 had given me hope that I was not too far off the beaten track.

Throughout my time in the air I had been quite oblivious to the absolute gentleness of the balloon. Now, though, as I began to descend with the softest of movements, the wonderful tranquility of the environment struck me. Never have I experienced such serenity. Surely this is a possible cure for many of the troubled people in the world. An afternoon of ballooning would be a tonic of unrivalled serenity. I find it difficult to imagine that drugs and/or assorted electrotherapy have anything to offer a vicious psychopath that an afternoon of solitude in a hot-air balloon could not provide in heapfuls. Rather than locking such people up only to subject them to an endless regime of chemicals and semi-torturous treatment, the answer is undoubtedly to get them into a balloon and set them free to wander the unbordered skies for a few hours or so. Of course it may be necessary to manacle to the basket those who might otherwise be tempted to drop themselves into people's gardens, but this is not such a significant difficulty. Howling might be more of a problem, particularly in residential areas.

Gradually approaching the layer of cloud, I wondered how this would affect the balloon. Would it be bumpy? I eyed the fluffy stuff with suspicion. It was now noticeably easier to breathe. Indeed, I was beginning to feel a rush of oxygen through my body and mind. Truly, ballooning is a wonderful affair! I vowed there and then to make it my hobby for the rest of my life. So are great decisions made. Some champagne, ideally Taittinger, would be the ideal companion.

As my breathing intensified, lungs gobbling up the thicker air, I began to encounter the first faint wisps of cloud. Quite intangible as they passed, they nevertheless made me aware of going through a barrier. For the first time I felt something like fear, instinctively dropping down into the basket and bracing myself. The light flashed and glimmered around me as the sun burst through occasional holes in the cloud fabric. Still there was no bump or resistance. I stood up and found myself in the cool comfort of cotton-wool heaven.

I came out of the clouds as abruptly as I had entered them. Below me, rolled out as far as I could see, was rocky ground: mottled brown canons and valleys, peaks and troughs. Nothing very civilized, though. At least, however, it was now possible to estimate how fast I was traveling by looking at those objects directly below. Judging from my initial sighting of a jagged spike of rock I was moving with some speed. Certainly I did not fancy touching down at this rate. But peering forwards I now found a greater concern. Ahead was a long range of mountains, dominating the horizon. I feared that it could be a matter of less than ten minutes before the balloon was upon them. Startled, I quickly set myself up for a burn and a rise over them. I slammed the "Ignition" button – and nothing happened.

Repeatedly I hammered the button but still nothing happened. Now I was desperate. At this rate I could see myself being bashed into the side of a mountain. There was no choice now but to get down on the ground. I pulled sharply on the yellow cord and held on. The balloon dropped abruptly and we started on a severe angle for the barren plain below.

On reflection I should have realized that there were layers of air, moving at different speeds and with different densities. This much is obvious when one considers the weather charts that are served up every day in newspapers and on television. Only one doesn't really understand the full depth of such charts' meaning until moving through the air itself. The balloon, which had previously been floating downwards as if supported by a band of cherubim, began lurching violently from side to side. Not only that, but the ground was now approaching at frightening speed. Too late I realized that far too much hot air had been expelled from the balloon. In desperation I tried again to re-ignite the gas ring, but to no avail. Looking down I spied a brief flash of rippling light ahead of me – water in one of the smaller valleys below. Then I was racing around the basket with all the control of Jack Russell terrier in the back seat of a car, throwing anything I could get my hands on out of the balloon in a woeful attempt to slow the descent. Three hundred feet. Deary, deary me. Two hundred feet. I threw up. One hundred feet. Yuck. Fifty. There was an almighty thump, my bobble hat flew off and I was hurled upside down into the bottom of the basket. A terrible screech filled the air and I realized with alarm that the envelope itself was not yet down and that basket was being dragged like a chariot across the rocky ground. With considerable effort I found and grasped the yellow cord, pulling and holding on to it with all my might, releasing the last of the air and so collapsing the envelope. With one final jerky skid we stopped and the basket fell over completely, violently spitting out me and everything else inside as the compartments released their contents. There was sharp crack as the burner unit hit the ground and snapped clear off the feeder pipe. I lay panting on my side, head hurting badly. With gentle apprehension I raised a finger to my crown, finding not blood but a nasty, sticky ooze. I gave it good sniff and was later to reflect on how fortunate it was that I should have come so far in such unfamiliar transport, landing with such abandon and yet end up lying on the ground, a vomit-covered head the only damage. I have been to lunch parties in South London with worse outcomes.

16. A Fresh Start

The middle of nowhere. I had been here before but always metaphorically. I must have passed out momentarily, coming to where I had fallen, still shocked and short of breath under various lines of rope, feeling like a fool. Eventually I unwrapped my arms, struggled upright and dusted myself down. Realizing that the balaclava was still on my head I ripped it off, throwing it away angrily, my face relishing the release. Damn! To have been flying so high and then to have lost it all through one ridiculous decision – how stupid.

A salesman must deal with stupidity on an almost daily basis. Most customers are incredibly stupid. The people you report to are invariably stupid. Your colleagues are, by and large, stupid. There is only you. If by some fluke you end up doing something stupid, walk away from it as quickly as possible. Find something to put your stupidity out of your mind. Your mind is your primary tool. Left to reflect on an act of stupidity, it will eat itself away, resulting in terminal self doubt. Walk into any fast-food establishment and you will find a self-doubting salesman, mind atwitch, suit creased, seeking comfort in a place where even he can still feel superior.

I picked through the debris of my belongings, strewn around the upturned balloon, looking for the water containers. Abruptly I remembered what I had seen from the balloon – a stretch of water. I knew immediately that I must go to it. The water would rid me of my stupidity. It is after all the great healer, the perfect end to any business day. A good enough dip can cleanse the filthiest soul. This is why a good swimming pool is a fundamental requirement of any business hotel. Many guests have spent the day involved in discussions or concluding deals which, while not being illegal or even immoral, will inevitably have about them elements of deceit. In Pontius Pilate's time a quick wash of the hands might have been sufficient. Nowadays a full half hour or so of swimming, with maybe ten minutes in the jacuzzi is necessary.

Find the water – it must be close now. I looked over my shoulder in the direction I had been heading. The plateau seemed to peak after a half mile or so. That had to be it. My body tingled at the thought of a good immersion.

From the surrounding mess I extricated a change of clothes, a towel and the toilet bag, laying the clothes out for my return. The temperature justified only a shirt and I looked forward to throwing off the thick layers that had kept me warm in the air. However, this would only be done immediately prior to entering the water in order to maximize the feeling of skins being shed. So, determined, I set off; towel tucked neatly under one arm, toilet bag under the other, to all the world like a law-abiding citizen on his way to a morning swim at the municipal leisure center.

"Purpose, purpose," I urged myself, striding briskly across the desolate plateau. Looking around me absently, there were few plants or shrubs to be seen; red earth and dust prevailed. I stopped to listen but, hearing nothing but the balmy wind, continued on my way, breaking open a pack of digestives I'd brought along for a snack. Ahead was the mountain range which had appeared so threatening but which I now realized was many, many miles away.

My legs moved with ease up the slope, even quickening slightly as the crest approached, feet digging in with each step, pushing upwards with determination. It was a long time since I had climbed a hill, indeed moved up any slope at all, and the movement itself was a pleasure. In particular, I enjoyed the stretching of the calf muscles with each step. At last I reached the peak, scrambling up the last few feet, arms flailing, before landing desperately on the point itself.

Some two hundred feet below me was the most wonderful river I had ever seen. The sides were gradual, allowing a deft paddle before full commitment with the body. The speed at which it moved looked excellent – there were few ripples and but the odd twist of white foam, indicating a firm, purposeful flow but not anything which might carry me off, naked and distressed.

I felt at my side for the toilet bag and towel and stood up. The way down to the river was exceptionally steep. I didn't fancy breaking a leg and decided to step down crab-style, giving myself a good edge against the slope. This cautious approach proved its wisdom immediately as my first foot downwards disappeared into the dust and kept sinking until my knee was covered. My heart sank equally as I realized that I would have to trudge back up through this and hence cover my clean body in fresh layers of the red dust. Nevertheless the lure of the water was too much and somewhat recklessly I started to descend with quick, adventurous steps and was soon going at a keen pace sideways down the slope. This same keen pace was what gave me lift when I hit a rock or something under the sand and shot out perpendicular to the incline, landing facedown and mobile. I gripped the toilet bag firmly. There was no stopping my speedy descent, much as I tried to with multiple limbs trashing. Dust was being forced into my nostrils and ears and I felt like I was burrowing ever downwards into the earth, the noise deafening as the sand rushed past. Suddenly – silence. I felt myself airborne and realized I was about to hit the river. I kept thrashing, such was my commitment.

Whoosh! I was in the water. Going down I was aware first of the wonderful novelty of clean water on my body; second, of the absolutely freezing temperature – this river was ice cold. The water seemed to fill every aspect of me. I surfaced gasping for air and in a state of some shock about twenty feet or so from the far bank. I started to breaststroke towards it as methodically as I could. This had to be water which had come direct from a mountain range. I was further chilled to think how alarming this swim would have been had the river flow been of any strength. I hauled myself onto the bank, sodden clothes resisting every move, and lay chattering violently for a couple of minutes, hugging my arms and legs. The faint heat of the day on my face prompted me to remove the clothes and give myself a good natural dry. I stood up, dancing from foot to foot with cold, and peeled off the various layers. These actions alone began the warming process and I was soon running naked round and round. After a few minutes I was completely out of breath and had to sit down. Nevertheless I felt much better. My temporary dip had not frozen me to the bone and now, sitting quietly under a warm, windless sky, I felt real again. Sliding facedown through the dust had given me a sort of intensive facial and my cheeks felt smooth as silk. Women would pay fortunes for that, I thought. So would men, now we're equal.

Seeing those old clothes lying there did indeed make me feel that a skin had been shed. Indeed, it seemed altogether like a butterfly day. I was mightily pleased to give my teeth a thorough brush. Putting the brush and toothpaste back into the toilet bag, I noticed with a sharp intake of breath a brand-new disposable razor at the bottom. I took it philosophically between thumb and forefinger, its absolute blueness entrancing me as I held it up to the horizon, turning it, taking in each angle. That I should stand here holding such an instrument seemed quite amazing. Were I to drop it, who knows when it might be found, or by whom. Religions could spring from it, cities be sacked, races neatly subdivided into those who recognized this razor as a holy artifact and those who rejected it. What power I now held. I stroked my chin, feeling a tough, thick beard. For the moment I would just have a shave.

Rummaging around further, I found a small bar of soap. I lay flat, at right angles to the river, with my head and chest overhanging the bank. On this occasion I decided not to shave upwards as the growth might be too strongly rooted. I scooped handfuls of freezing water up and rubbed it into my beard. I had never had a beard before and it was odd to think that I had been living life for some time as a bearded man. I myself had been largely unaware of having had one during this time. In what sense was I a bearded man, then? I thought. Still wondering, I soaked the soap briefly in the river, working up a solid lather which I rubbed deep into the bristles, eventually working the bar up and down the neck, chin and cheeks as the size of the job at hand became clearer – this could be tough. I gave the whole thing a great working over, then took the plastic cover off the razor, placed it high on my left cheek and began to pull down slowly, pushing the blade firmly against the skin. Surely, steadily I cut my first swathe. What joy as it cleared its path. Naturally the blades clogged up quicker than when clearing a mere day of growth. Furthermore, halfway through I had to lather up all over again as simple soap does not retain its moisturizing function as well as a good shaving cream. Yet even allowing for these factors it was a great, great shave, possibly my best ever. With each completed run I would move my palm down the cleared area. After no more than twenty minutes I stood shaking excess water from my face. Inspired, I bent down and thrust my head fully under the water, my skin shrieking at the cold. It took three full duckings before I was able to get anything like a decent soap-up as my head was absolutely filthy, with much of the hair firmly stuck to the scalp. Soon enough, though, I was running round and round again, head shaking, whooping lightly in my beautiful nakedness. This was a man who was ready to battle the world. This was a man who would find his way home. This was a man with a mission.

I have often pondered subsequently on how a good shave and cold head-wash can transform one's mood and perspective entirely. Sadly most women will never know the joy of a deep and methodical shave. Perhaps there is a market for some product – nylon filings in light glue maybe – which women could sprinkle on their faces in time of need, to experience the catharsis of the facial shave. Perhaps they might also then understand the male psyche better.

I sat down to collect myself. Hunger was setting in and it was time to get back to the balloon for food and sleep. Considering how best to do so I spotted the toilet bag bobbing in a rivulet. I must have knocked it in absentmindedly. I rushed to retrieve it and, fishing it out of the water, experienced a revelation. In general, revelations are to be avoided. Particularly in business, where they can mark you out as difficult. But seeing the little toilet bag bobbing gently in the water gave me a jolt. This was the way back. As sure as man loves woman, civilization is attracted to water. This river would undoubtedly be home to countless villages and towns – at the very end there was bound to be a city. And I would bob my way down to it in the balloon basket. Then it would simply be a case of abandoning ship somewhere and making my way to the nearest British Embassy with a suitable tale of international intrigue. How that might run was not of immediate concern. All that mattered now was that the way forward was clear. When the way forward is clear, details can be added when needed.

17. PREPARATIONS

I tucked the toilet bag under my arm and plunged back into the icy water and soon lay panting on the opposite bank. Climbing the steep hill itself must have taken the best part of two hours, as the thick sand ate up my every step, turning each lunge forwards into an inexorable slide back. Yet throughout this stage I was careful not to fall into self-pity. Self-pity is the grave of many a would-be salesman. Sometimes things can get too much. It is true that, sitting in a luridly decorated, cheap hotel room, a beige polyester quilt cover the only companion after a day of cancelled orders, the bar long closed, one can begin to feel sorry for oneself. This is when the daily telephone call back to HQ can be so important.

A good sales director will be able to detect the downward trend of his stay and deal with it effectively. The solution is relatively simple: replace Self-Pity with Fear. For example:

SALESMAN: I have tried so very hard and yet the sales slip through my fingers like grains of sand. What have I done to merit this injustice?

SALES DIRECTOR: Listen, matey – get your monthly quota on time, fullyconfirmed by Friday noon latest. This is not an organization that employs, or gives references for, work-shy failures. If you don't deliver you might as well kill yourself.

Most salesmen are unwilling to kill themselves and as such will be sure to get the order in as required. Resolve is a matter of hunger. Make people hungry enough and they will do anything.

Thus, from the moment I stepped into the river for the swim back, I flooded my mind with images of the life that had been stolen from me. There was the understated elegance of the well-timed automatic smoked-glass door at the hotel entrance, the knowledgeable bustle and chatter of the foyer, the rigid smile of the receptionists, their delightfully scripted pattern of English usage, the full-frontal servility of the bagboy. Again and again these thoughts rallied me, urged me on. My head was awash with the sights, sounds and smells of the international business traveling life. It was this kaleidoscope of velour curtains, padded coat hangers and pygmy shampoo bottles that served as a vision towards which I climbed, stumbling, falling but without once doubting my cause.

Back at the landing site the task was clear. There was no way of knowing how well the basket would float. In order to ensure maximum bobbage in the river a simple precaution would be to leave behind all unnecessary items. I surveyed the spewed-out belongings, spread out across the ground like a jumble sale. There were a lot of clothes, enough food for about two weeks, a sleeping bag, a medical kit, more toiletries and, previously unnoticed, a cassette player (two sets of batteries) and a small collection of tapes. Three of these were marked "Country and Western Various," in Anthony's handwriting, a fourth as "Johnny Cash – From Dad" in firm black capitals, and a fifth "For Those Lonesome Moments Love Your Mother" in curly red felt tip. What thoughtful parents. Some books had been wrapped in towels: a thick medical dictionary, a compact paperback edition of the complete works of Jane Austen, a large atlas, a handbook on agrarian economics. Finally a brand-new hardback – *My Life for the Poor: Mother Teresa of Calcutta,* by José Gonzalez and Janet N. Playfoot. Nearest to the balloon, and obviously what had been at the unexplored bottom of the compartments, were a number of implements.

Put together it was an entire camping cooking set: pots and pans, knives and forks and so forth, with a small gas cooker. Finally a few personal Anthony items. A framed photograph of him with his mother and father – an awkward and heavy item to take along on a voyage round the world – along with various lucky charms: rabbit's paw, St. Christopher's medallion, silver spoon and so forth.

Clearly all the food was required, as was the sleeping bag, medical kit and so forth. The cooking stuff would be needed, but only one pan and one plate and a couple of water containers. As for the clothes, these were easily sorted. One exceptionally warm overlaying "emergency" outfit was required to augment a set of four everyday changes: T-shirts and the like, which could be easily washed and dried. I indulged myself with a pair of corduroy trousers which, judging from their wrapped condition, had obviously been intended for use on indeterminate "dressy" occasions. Corduroy has always had something of a mystic quality for me. The tight ribs give a structured feel that cannot be found in any other fabric. Velvet, while similarly plush, lacks this discipline. Corduroy comes from the phrase "Cord of Kings" and more people would do well to recognize its moral value. A world where corduroy was the textile of choice would be truly a noble place.

The tape player and tapes would be nice to have along. As for the books, I would not know what to do with the medical text; Jane Austen is a load of twaddle; agrarian economics was of no interest either – some scribbling in the margins indicated that this was Anthony's study material for a productive return to Ohio; Mother Teresa never did anything for me. No, the books could all go. As could the family portrait. As could the lucky charms, if not for the weight issue then because they clearly did not work. Never take lucky charms from bodies. Finally, the envelope itself was clearly unnecessary, although I would take three of the ropes, neatly coiled.

Nevertheless, even having released the fuel tanks and discarded as much as possible, the combined weight of the basket and contents was a heavy proposition. There was little choice but to make two journeys to the river – one for my possessions, another for the basket. With no other container I had to place the retained items in the sleeping bag and deposit this luggage at the edge of the river prior to beginning the haul of the basket itself.

Luggage was a polite term for a sleeping bag full of stolen goods. Yet even thinking of it as my luggage made me feel better. Luggage always gives a wonderful sense of purpose, of destiny. Patting one's suitcases as one waits for the arrival of the airport taxi has about it the air of the cowboy patting his trusty steed.

Returning for the basket, I picked over the abandoned pile of items to check that nothing of any import had been overlooked. A couple of knives were picked up. About to leave, I spontaneously threw the Mother Teresa book into the basket too. Such is the way with modern travel – you always end up reading about things you never expect to.

It took the best part of the day to drag the balloon basket to the top of the incline. Each step was bitter agony, the edges digging deeply into the soft dirt, the basket still heavy despite being empty. In moving the basket, though, I became aware of the amazing changes in my own body. I was significantly wirier, less flabby, more succinct in frame. I would even go so far as to say "healthier." The relative lack of alcohol, coupled with the consumption of meat-free, vegetable-based meals, might well have produced a significant difference on their own. Add to this the prodigious amount of walking, carrying, sweating, and it was no surprise that I should feel so physically changed.

The original concept, formed while moving the basket, had been for it and me to slide toboggan-style down the slope, landing bottom side down in the river in one graceful sliding motion. Again, the soft sandy soil interfered. I had to march the basket down the hill, swinging the front corners forward in turn – left, right, left, right. Each movement required me to heave the structure out of the sand. Lumbering slowly down to the water, I felt like one of the earliest would-be land-dwelling leviathans, defeated by my time ashore and now plodding with resignation back to my true home.

I woke before dawn. Many nights spent in a drunken coma on a cold bathroom floors have taught me that the coldest time, that point when the heat of day has most dissipated, is about 5 a.m. It is generally then that one's body forces the issue, waking you to demand warmth. On this occasion I had not wrapped myself properly before sleep, simply falling where I arrived, half in and half out of the basket. Having dragged it for the best part of the day across the plain and then down the slope and then across the river, I had collapsed as the sun set and was now both ravenous and cold even as the first vestiges of sunrise were washing the horizon. I crawled into the basket, pulled over the protective sheet and wrapped myself tightly in the sleeping bag, pawing around blindly for some energy snacks. These I devoured before falling under once more.

During this second sleep I had a dream. The picture was of me floating down the river in the balloon basket. This was an inspiring picture; I was clearly in control, standing in the middle of the basket, hands firmly on the bow, my eyes narrowing as I regarded the approaching water with easy contempt. I had a clean pair of socks on to indicate to the world how confident I was that no mere river water was capable of breaching my plastic domain. What a proud sight I made.

My plan was thus easily formulated. I would drag the basket with contents to the river. At the river the basket would turn into a boat and I would float into the next village or town. In such cases it was usual for some small children or women washing by the river to spot the incoming stranger and then to run ahead to alert the townspeople. It was therefore by no means unlikely that I would soon be greeted by a hail of flowers of all colors spilt from carrier bags held aloft on bridges. Babies on men's shoulders would soon be pointing at my passing craft. I wondered if there were a sufficient number of colored T-shirts and underwear to create a good standard of bunting. If I had some chocolate left I would undoubtedly hand it out to the helpful waifs who would guide me to the shore. Then it would be a simple matter of telephoning in for an airborne rescue before settling down to the banquet prepared by the whole village, covertly returning at some point to the basket and releasing it, the only evidence, to float off downstream. In dealing with the villagers I would not, however, let myself be paraded round the village on the back of some mangy donkey, something they would probably want to do with a glamorous stranger who arrives unexpectedly. I would, politely, decline the donkey.

18. AFLOAT

Dreams are important tools for sales management. Nightmares, too. As the experienced salesman knows, asking for their "dream scenario" is an ideal opener with a difficult client. Clients love nothing more than spluttering on about this sort of thing and it gives the salesman the opportunity to pick up all sorts of tidbits that can be inserted into the subsequent sales pitch. Nightmares work on a different principle. Nightmares are what you implant in reluctant clients when you're leaving. For example:

SALESMAN: John, I'm breaking all the rules here, but whether you can afford this unit or not doesn't really come into it. I know that your top three competitors have already placed their orders, either with us or with one of our rivals. Anyway, I won't trouble you any more with such nightmares. See you soon.

CLIENT: *(Nervous now)* OK, bye.

Two or three day later you'll get the call. If all else fails, interfering with someone's sleep patterns – giving them nightmares to envisage – is the best way to continue the sales pitch after you've gone. People forget offers and discounts. They can't forget waking up every night, shivering with fear.

That morning I was alive to my dream. I soon had the basket packed and moored in the river. Looking over my abandoned pile of clothing from that first swim, I decided to take along the jumpsuit. Made as it was of some sort of waterproof stuff, it might afford a degree of protection should conditions get rougher. I untied the basket from the bank and, holding the rope, walked out to it, naked up to my waist. As I threw the rope in I felt the basket move ever so slightly. Scrambling over the side seemed to do the trick, for even as I picked myself up from the bottom there was undoubtedly movement. As I stood, the landscape was now passing softly by. I waved to it and called, "Goodbye! Goodbye!" I was on the final stage home.

It would have been nice to have had a camera with me. Generally speaking I avoid photography and anyone connected with it. Hotels are full of people who appear to have little to do all day but go here and there taking photographs of things. Who cares where you've been – someone else has always been there before you. Who cares what you see – you can see it again if you really want to. The only people who take photographs of "sights" are those for whom life is a bleak tunnel with but the occasional burst of light. In other words, people who at the end of their run will have a few mixed views of foreign places they passed through as a summary of what they did of interest. Of course, in this respect perhaps, the photographing of sights is not without its own kind of courage.

For five days I saw absolutely nothing of any note. I watched with wry disinterest as all manner of strange-looking rock formations and the occasional absurd plant or tree went by on either side. But no people – no civilizations – no hotels. Each night I would tie a rope round my waist and swim ashore, then heave the basket into the shallows, moor it and make dinner. I would sleep in the basket, preferring to be swept away in it than left behind. By the sixth day I had started listening to Country and Western music and by the seventh was reading about Mother Teresa. I would sit in the bottom of the basket, read about one hundred words, then get up to see if anything was looming. By the eighth day I had stopped getting up altogether, content to rely on the motion of the basket and my ears to warn of anything untoward. This meant I was no longer able to listen to any music.

Mother Teresa is not her real name, of course. It is her *nom de plume,* or *nom de pauvre,* if you will. She was born Agnes Gonxha Bojaxhiu in Albania in 1910, the daughter of a grocer. She decided, apparently, to become a missionary at the age of twelve. This seemed an absurdly young age to decide something so momentous. How could anyone decide to lead such a life without understanding the alternatives? Even then there were other careers for women. She could have done worse than become a grocer herself.

As a teenager I once decided to search for God, although I only got as far as watching television through the window of a rental shop at the local shopping center. Some might find this "ironic" or "chillingly appropriate." I know it was just laziness. Nowadays I only encounter God in the odd cry of "Oh God!" from a neighboring hotel room, usually one of desperation rather than sexual ecstasy. Occasionally at close of play in a bar, one will find a group of tie-undone businessmen talking about religion and belief, although they typically deny it the next day. There is always one atheist hammering on, demanding Proof. I do find it odd that atheists insist on Absolute Proof. As anyone who has ever loved or pursued a woman will tell you, it is in the tease and hint that passion is aroused. That is what a real God would do: flirt with us, using disputable miracles and indeterminate actions.

Mother Teresa not only believed in God, she felt his will. After joining the Sisters of Loreto, a community of nuns in Dublin, she founded the first "Pure Heart" shelter for the dying in India in 1952 and later a leper colony near Asanol, partly funded by a raffle for a car donated by Pope Paul VI. All along she felt that God wanted her to be with the poor. She went into the streets of Calcutta with only five rupees, giving four to some poor people and one to a priest. The same priest later brought her a further fifty rupees. Her first contact was a dying woman, her body chewed by rats, whom the local hospital refused to admit. Mother Teresa insisted.

I imagine that Mother Teresa would have made a good salesman. Not one like me, the careful, deal-oriented, learn-plan-execute type. No, Mother Teresa would have belonged to the old school – get in there, put your briefcase quietly down and make it quite clear that you would not be leaving without an order. I have occasionally resorted to this tactic myself but it is not my day-to-day method of operation.

As far as Mother Teresa was concerned, there were two kinds of poverty, one material, the other spiritual. This struck me at the time as being quite true. But I was immediately distracted from this moment by a flash of light, or rather a shadow, as something passed overhead. Looking up, startled, I saw a large, predatory-looking bird reel off into the hills. I stood up to watch it and then, turning downriver, found myself staring at the outline of a small village. Elated, I dropped the book and prepared for civilization and hopefully a drink.

19. SAVING

There are few things worse than to arrive and not be greeted. My arrival in the village went completely unnoticed and this was most disappointing. There had not been, apparently, any child scouts on the hilltops, nor any trained raccoon-family animals in the undergrowth tied to pieces of string that were in turn tied to little hand-crafted bells. I came into the settlement quite unheralded, to a welcome of profound silence. Yet even this could not diminish my excitement at finally being "somewhere." The "where" of this was the last important bit. Most places on the face of the earth cherish broadly the same comforts. The appeal of the foreign is largely one of not knowing the word for "bathroom." After that it's all pretty much the same, give or take the odd item of tableware.

I tied up the basket opposite the first hut. The lack of basic pleasantries made me cautious, suspicious even. Perhaps the wily villagers were up tom something. The basket floated invitingly behind me and I toyed with the idea of simply getting back in and continuing along to the next town. After a moment of such contemplation I recognized this as nonsense – here was what I had been looking for: civilization, albeit rudimentary.

Nevertheless, seeing that the village petered out about five hundred yards further down – there was what appeared to be a drinking and washing station midway through – I deiced that I would prefer to moor on the downriver side. This would permit a quick exit if need be. On reflection I think that this preference was much to do with my extensive flying experience as anything else. It is always better to get the seat which allows you to get on and off as quickly as possible, meaning that you can arrive late and leave early, thus minimizing the time available for cabin bores to gnaw away any respect you have left for fellow passengers.

One of the more bizarre things about in-flight conversations is the scale to which complete strangers are desperate to reveal all manner of details of their private or business lives. It's like being trapped inside an airborne confessional. While I am happy to endure the odd tale of marital infidelity or family abandonment, perhaps even provoke it, I am less than happy to learn about various corporate activities, such as impending deals or likely tie-ups. This is not because of the content but because of the sense of betrayal. If one is not loyal to one's company, if one is willing to use national strategies and the like as mere titillation among fellow business-class passengers, then one is not worthy of the corporate badge. The next time someone reveals all to you concerning their company's operations, write it all down after. Then send it anonymously to the company's managing director, enclosing the business card of the chump concerned (chumps love nothing more than giving out their business cares). The last time I followed this course of action a phone call one month later revealed that the disloyal executive was no longer with the company. Quite right, too. The business life is not a game; it is a mission. Destroy all infidels.

I moored the basket about fifty feet outside the village on the other side, concealed behind an outcrop of rock. Before leaving it I changed into the corduroy trousers, which fitted me rather well. First impressions do count. I then considered whether or not I should take anything else along. This was clearly not an advanced society – there were no signs of telephone lines or aerials of any sort. It was most probably some sort of agrarian affair, with the odd bit of inter-valley barter for a bit of seasonal "when the moon is full" excitement. The type of place which *National Geographic* likes to find and preserve so that they've got something to write about.

Such a primitive setup would surely appreciate a gift. I fished out the tape recorder and inserted one of the cassettes; Johnny Cash would do. I checked around me for anyone watching, then padded my way back along the riverbank to the other side.

I was about thirty feet from the nearest building, with a track going into the village some fifty yards further to my left. I walked quickly over and on to it, then turned towards the settlement. There was no need for anyone to know that I'd arrived by water.

My gait was refined, assured, confident. I was now firmly inside the perimeter but could still see no one. I stopped and listened. Nothing. I moved to the doorway of the nearest hut. The structure was built entirely of long canes bound together. It looked quickly collapsible. I knocked on the door, which was simply lying against the opening. No answer. I stepped back, deciding not to enter. The path led further into the village and I followed it for another few yards before hearing what sounded like a lone voice a little way off. Listening closely, it seemed that someone was speaking clearly and without distraction, like a lecture of some kind. I moved towards the voice—not English, more flowing – now creeping from hut to hut, getting closer to what was clearly the sound of one man speaking in carefully measured tones. Perhaps the village chief or the local shaman, I thought, crouching behind a large pile of sticks – firewood? I crept quietly forwards until the beginnings of a throng were visible. Peering round, it was clear that this was no untidy rabble. At the rear, their erect backs to me, stood the tallest men; in front of them, the not so tall men; in front of them, seated or kneeling on the ground, I could just make out the village's women. An organized assembly of some neatness. I eased around further. Their skin was brown, although no more "brown" than my own was now. Not too tall. Hair tied up for the most part, universally black in color. So I was still somewhere in Asia. A T-shirt designer in Tokyo once explained to me how much easier it is to create and style for a market in which one knows with almost absolute certainty the hair color of most of the population, in a way that is seldom encountered in Western society. I have oft had cause to reflect on this when considering the dearth of coordination in the business-class queue at most European airports. If we were to adopt a calendar approach, whereby hair colors were agreed in advance, this would surely result in a significant improvement to our fashion heritage.

Through tightly-packed shoulders the speaker could be seen facing the crowd; a middle-aged man with a thin moustache, dressed in the same utilitarian dusty plain cottons as the other men, was striding up and down in a declamatory manner, supporting his words with a fine display of exuberant hand and body language. I was reminded of a Pakistani customs official and his attempts to get me to release my grip on a bottle of Cutty Sark while his colleagues forcibly strip-searched me. Perhaps that was where I was – Pakistan. The fact that I could not place their tongue as Urdu was neither here not here. The number of dialects and regional variations in this part of the globe is a source of constant wonder. As such I find it by far the best policy to ignore what people are saying until they start speaking English. Most officials seem able to get the word "Stop" out before any serious damage is done.

Ceasing suddenly, he pointed dramatically at something to his right-hand side, at which point most of the crowd seemed to clap and cheer enthusiastically. I stood on tiptoe. On the far left, flanked on either side by a single man, was a wooden cage and in this cage, a woman, clad in a wraparound affair which did not distinguish her from the others. This was a trial.

The woman looked remarkably unrepentant, although I supposed she might not have been guilty. It must, though, have been some particularly nasty crime to have the village gathered like this. There was little to see in the way of what might be called evidence; certainly no body or harmed person was laid out anywhere. Neither were the two guards conspicuously armed. All this seemed to point to a non-violent social crime of some sort – something white-collar. Meanwhile the speech continued. I wondered if there might be anything in the way of a kiosk dispensing food and alcohol. Events such as this often bring out stalls and the like.

I continued to move round. Surely there would be alcohol. Some years back I had read an article which stated authoritatively that there were no people anywhere on the face of the earth that did not have an alcoholic beverage of some sort. I can still remember the beauty of that day as my face rose from the printed page – I could go anywhere! So here and now in this village I had one of two things for sure. Either alcohol or a genuine anthropological discovery. Discoveries are of no use to me and I prayed that these people were as mundane as everybody else.

I was considering all of this when it hit me very hard that I was wasting my time. Wasting time is not something any self-respecting salesman ever does. Consider two examples where a salesman is clearly wasting his time.

CUSTOMER: Is it possible to go through your price structure again? I need to understand how you arrive at these figures.

SALESMAN: I'm going to have to ask you to appreciate that our price structure is our price structure. It is not a matter where discussion can benefit either of us in the long run. Perhaps we could meet up again once you've had time to consider your position.

In other words, our prices are our prices. If you don't like them, go elsewhere. Many customers have a mistaken understanding of what bargaining is about. Similarly women, as in the following telephone conversation.

MAN: So would you like to go out for a drink tonight?

WOMAN: I'm not sure. What time did you have in mind?

Man hangs up telephone.

This is going nowhere. Prevarication or indecision is never an acceptable answer to yes/no questions. If she wants to go out for a drink – fine; if she doesn't – fine. It's her life. Your time.

I had been in the village for some time now without receiving any calculable benefit. Action was required. I took the tape recorder in my hand and marched out into full view. "Hello!" I shouted, and pressed "Play." The crowd looked at me bubble-eyed with apprehension, then amazement as the first chords of "A Boy Named Sue" wafted spirit-like into the gathering. There was a single shriek and then a stampede. Shortly thereafter I realized, amid a cloud of dust, that I was alone. Apart from the captured woman who sat in the farthest corner of the cage, watching me in rigid terror. I approached, arms wide apart, in peace. She screamed. Instinctively looking around, I caught the vanishing tops of so many nervous heads ducking behind huts. Turning back to the terrified woman, I switched off Johnny Cash.

 Silence. I stood next to the cage and gave the international sign for "drink" – a cupped hand seesawing back and forth against the lips. She said something timidly and pointed with one shaking hand. Following her finger I realized that she meant the village's drinking station on the river. Again I gave the sign for "drink," this time adding a swaying, stumbling body motion; the sign for inebriation. The woman's brow furrowed and she moved forwards slightly, crouching. I continued my demonstration. Again she moved forward, right up against the door of the cage. My drink dance went on. Suddenly her hand flashed outside the bars and released the clasp. In a blur the door swung open and caught me full in the face. I yelped and collapsed to my knees, watching as the woman careered out of the village and away into the low foothills beyond. I had only wanted a drink.

Nursing my nose, I became aware of a shuffling noise behind. Turning around, I found the whole population of the village creeping towards me. I snapped Johnny Cash back on and they retreated. Holding the tape recorder in front of me, I moved towards them – determined to extract something from this visit. They backed off at speed. I reached the first hut and ducked inside, scanning the interior with haste, emerging a matter of seconds later to find that the crowd had once more advanced towards me. There was a degree of muttering among them now and I felt their fear ebbing. It could only be a matter of minutes. A second hut yielded nothing other than a mother holding her child protectively, in a somewhat predictable Sunday supplement pose. I leaped into a third hut – success! In the corner was a pair of gourds, strung together at the neck. I grabbed them and got out, backing with authority towards the clearing. The crowd now came on. I swung the gourds in their hide containers over my shoulder and step by step reached the point at which it would be necessary to make a run for the river. It was then, when I needed him most, that Johnny came to the end of "A Boy Named Sue." I stood still; they stopped, before beginning slowly but surely to inch forwards. The silence was my death knell. Abruptly, with an almighty krang that shocked me into dropping the tape player, the opening chords of "Folsom Prison Blues" blew the villagers' new-found courage away. They backed off, reeling from the fresh assault. Now was the time for action. I placed the tape recorder on the ground, then ran with all my might into the water, surging towards the basket. Glancing back I could see a crowd gathering tentatively round the music. Rapidly freeing the basket, I heaved it downstream and towards the body of the river before hauling myself over the side, gasping and shattered.

Apprehension made me stand to check that a safe getaway had been achieved. The village was now quietly receding, the crowd no more than a spot. As the current took me swiftly on, I turned to face forwards. Doing so, I found myself eye to eye with another inhabitant of the village. Certainly he was dressed the same way, although his clothes were in some ways less grubby, more respectable. He stood on the bank in front of what was clearly a rudimentary cross, holding a thick book, open in the middle. As we passed directly opposite one another he looked down at his book, startled, then up again. In a voice cracking with wonder he called, "Moses?" I waved languidly and the river swept me away.

20. Exodus

I regretted the loss of the tape recorder. Country and Western is never my favorite but I missed the idea of music in general. It whets the appetite for life. The sacrifice of the music, and my possible near death at the hands of the villagers, had nevertheless been worth it. Nestling in the corner of my basket were two skin containers filled with alcohol. There must have been nearly six liters in total.

From then on I avoided villages. What was the point? No, my goal was a city. A city with business hotels; a city of life. Obviously I would not be able to return immediately to my corporate existence. An explanation would need to be provided for my unexpected absence. Yet in this respect, the right explanation would be no explanation. Why? Because in cases where a difficult explanation is the only other option, severe amnesia is to be preferred. For example:

SALES DIRECTOR: Did you or did you not promise Williams Machinery Ltd a twenty percent discount?

SALESMAN: I'm pretty sure I didn't.

SALES DIRECTOR: Yes or no? Williams swears blind that you did.

SALESMAN: To be honest, I can't remember.

Notice the beauty of the last line, allowing yourself to "be honest" and at the same time lie.

My story would run something like this:

Having accompanied Elizabeth back to my hotel, I decide to have a nightcap on my own. The hotel bar is unappealing so I venture out preferring not to hand over my key. It is often better to keep hold of one's room key, particularly if the receptionists are of the type for whom English is not so much a foreign language as an attempt on their life. Ensconced in a local bar – the Hungry Panther is always packed – I find myself in conversation with a couple Malayan businessmen (never blame the host country). Leaving a couple of hours later, I feel faint at the door and collapse, only to find the supporting arms of the Malayan businessmen under me as I fall. They offer to drop me at my hotel. Getting into their black Mercedes (plenty in Bangkok) is the last thing I am able to remember, having woken, confused and penniless, in whatever city I finally arrive in. White slavery investigation follows. No need to mention the kidnapping. No need to mention the balloon. I resume my life.

So I floated on. At each occasional passing of a village I would try to shimmy the basket towards the far side of the river, then duck down to avoid causing undue excitement while I passed. At night I camped on land. And now I had some alcohol to steady me. It was a vicious starch-based spirit, evil-smelling but quite acceptable once diluted with a little water, although at first it made me throw up. Each night would end, each day begin, with a celebratory swig as I felt my journey moving towards a happy conclusion. I had some before lunch, too.

Gradually the banks of the river took more and more effort to reach. By now I had scooped up a drifting plank and was using it to paddle and steer as best as possible. The river was clearly widening as it progressed. Here and there I could see streams and smaller rivers flowing into it, adding to its might. I knew that it could not be long before I came to a city. Then came the day when I realized that it would not be possible to stop for the night. Getting over to either bank proved impossible. Still I did not worry. When the time came I would simply swim for shore, using the plank as a flotation aid if need be.

So it was in a mood of high spirits one day that I decided to treat myself to a special drink or two. I had just finished lunch and, now being able to picture most vividly how my plight would play out, unstopped the heavier of the two gourds. The sun was particularly strong that day and I pulled the basket cover over, fished out my mug and gave one of the gourds a firm pump. Total, pleasant inebriation followed.

In any life there comes a time when your closest friend lets you down. It may be at a party, in the supermarket or on the beach. For me it occurred in the middle of a river, approaching the ocean. At some point that afternoon I passed out. But this was not a normal passing out, such as I had previously encountered three or four times a week for the past twenty years. This was a special one. Towards the end of the session I can dimly recall drinking the spirit straight – the water had run out and I couldn't be bothered reaching over the side for more – which probably didn't help.

I only came to at all because of the deafening sound of a ship's horn nearby. I jumped to my feet, ripping the cover open. It was night. About one hundred yards away from me was an enormous tanker, side-on, passing me by. It blew its horn again and the basket shuddered. I looked all around. On either side were the lights of a town, no, a city. But they were clearly several miles away. In between were the silhouettes of tens of ships, each ploughing with purpose either into or out of port. I tired calling out but my voice was lost amid the clank and throb of so many engines. I was drifting out to sea and at speed. The river had now acquired an unquenchable desire to be free, to roam at will, with me strapped to its back. Even the strongest of swimmers could not have made the shore against such a current. I shouted and shrieked but to no effect, finally collapsing distraught into the basket. Somewhere, under a soft, golden light, a large gin and tonic was being placed on a marble counter by a well-shaven mid-thirties bartender in a black waistcoat. But not for me.

21. JOURNEY'S END

The lurch was almost over. For most of my life I had lurched from bed to table, table to table, to bar, to bed. Now this lurch was about to end. I had been drifting at sea for four days. My lips were baked to a hard crust. My head throbbed constantly. I had lost the basket cover on the first day. Waving it wildly, in a futile bid to entice faraway ships, it had slipped from my grip through sheer exhaustion, shooting out into the water. It was then that I saw the first gray fin, circling the floating cover, which abruptly vanished from sight in a flurry of water. An industrial salvage diver had once, over an evening of martinis, explained how sharks are attracted to the channels and currents in and out of ports, as these inevitably contain all sorts of discarded tidbits. So for three days I had been cooked by the sun, trying to conceal myself in basket corners, each time the waves gently turning the basket to expose my hiding place. The final damnation had come when, trying to drink some of the village alcohol on a stomach desperate for water, I was reduced to convulsions as my body reeled and squealed in dry agony. I had thrown the gourds overboard, wretched and weeping.

All good salesmen can recognize the end. Occasionally their recognition is audible, as they tumble past your balcony on the way to the ground. The end does not mean failure. It means that life itself has come to an end. When the sale that must be got cannot be got, it is all over, like the old bird that isn't quick enough to grab the worms any more. The night there was a storm and the next morning my head was bleeding from being bashed on the side of the basket. Worse still, the basket was about one-quarter filled with water. I changed into the jumpsuit as it at least afforded some protection from the sun without being too hot or absorbing water. I then set about bailing out the basket with a cooking pot although I kept passing out myself.

Some birds had taken to floating nearby – albatrosses, I think. One of them came very close and in a fit of strength I cast the Mother Teresa book, heavy with water, down on to it, catching it square on the head. It keeled over. Then the long, straight wings extended slowly from its upturned body so that it resembled an old man asleep in front of the fire, head resting on the chair back. A pleasure I would never know.

I can faintly recall a fresh wind blowing over the basket in gentle relief from the midday heat, the ocean shimmering. Then I thought that I could actually see some dark bird descend from on high, perhaps a friend of the albatross, come to take me to the final destination. Then nothing.

22. PURGATORY

"Honey, it'll be fine."

A man's voice. The sound of someone crying.

"Honey, it'll be fine."

The sound of quiet, joyful tears.

Gradually feeling, awareness, returned. Pressure on my body. Light, comforting, even pressure; a tightly sheeted bed. My head on a pillow. Complete darkness. Body felt bulky, strange. My face could not move – something was holding it in place. I tried to speak – a rasping gurgle.

"Anthony, Anthony!" a woman's voice wailed, trembling with emotion.

"Son – take it easy – don't strain yourself. It's all right. I'll get the doctor." The man's voice. A door opening and closing. Footsteps down a corridor. There was a slight pressure, someone sitting gently on the end of the bed, and the weeping resumed. I lay in silence, feeling that my hands were wrapped in cotton, greasy, covered in some way. And I couldn't move it. Something was attached to my arm – a drip, I presumed. Footsteps approaching down the corridor, more than had left. The door opened.

"Oh Doctor, Doctor – he must be suffocating." The woman's voice, terrified.

Now a measured voice, male, reassuring, calm; perhaps a slight accent.

"Mrs. Hislop, your son has perhaps awoken briefly. Nothing more. He is not suffocating, of that I can assure you. Perhaps we can ask him?" A slight, confident suggestion. Deliberative hush, then: "Anthony, Anthony, can you hear us?" A concerned mother. I decided to bide my time.

"Anthony, your mother and father are here. Everything is all right." The doctor now, more affirmative. I waited. The doctor was foreign, his English pronunciation too pristine to be that of a native speaker.

"Anthony, we're here for you, your mother and I." A heartfelt father's touch. They deserved something. I gave a slight gurgle. The room broke in relief. The bed sprung upwards – the mother must have got up now to hug me or something. The doctor held her back, saying, "Wait, Mrs. Hislop! Please don't. Anthony's skin is still in a very sensitive state. I must ask you to refrain from touching him. He knows you're both here and that is what is most important right now."

There was more weeping, with both parents saying "Son, son," and "Oh Anthony." I said or gurgled no more.

After a further hour or so of sitting with me, Mr. and Mrs. Hislop left, urged on their way by the kindly doctor. I was most relieved, as the weeping was beginning to upset me. Overt displays of emotions are disturbing at the best of times. They had been sitting on the end of the bed while I pretended to be asleep. Every now and then Mrs. Hislop would move to touch me and Mr. Hislop would restrain her, "Not yet, dear, not yet, dear," and she would sit back again. "My son, my son." During this time I confirmed to my own satisfaction that I was wrapped to the point of immobilization from head to toe in bandages, with a hole under my nostrils for air. Leaving, they said, "Goodbye Anthony, we'll be back home before you know it," in an upbeat, jazzy way quite inconsistent with the previous bedside misery, and I detected the counseling hand of the kindly doctor.

Time passed. Perhaps two hours. It was impossible to tell. Two more people came in. An indifferent female voice said,

"Apparently he woke up this afternoon. The instructions are that we should take more care now."

I felt the bedclothes being pulled back. A pair of hands on each side of me now worked together to strip my bottom half. As they did so I realized I was wearing a large nappy. This was removed and the other person, again female, said, "Golly gosh – what a smell today!" and they both laughed. I was then turned on my front and given a bed bath.

"Are you awake, Anthony?"

I gurgled lightly.

"How are you feeling?"

I gurgled again, trying to put some variation in the tone.

"It's not so bad, is it? You'll maybe get your mouth opened tomorrow. That's what Dr. Patel said anyway."

I made appreciative noises.

"You'd like that, would you? Well, we'll be happier when you're strong enough to get to the bathroom on your own, won't we?"

The other one giggled merrily. How strong was I? I had no idea. Indeed, I knew nothing about how long I had been here or where "here" was. There was only one thing I did know –

everyone was convinced that I was Anthony Hislop, balloon pilot. I alone knew that the real Anthony Hislop was probably dead by now, having expired midway through a burial quest that he thought would free his soul from Limbo. A burial quest initiated by me. And although I was in no doubt that my membership of the Mackenzie Industrial family entitled me to use of the balloon, equally there could be no doubt that if all was revealed it would be me that would be cast as villain.

I was woken the next day and given a nappy change; two different nurses who said little other than "How's the famous balloon pilot then?" Each time, before the nappy went back on, my mid-regions were smeared extensively with a cold, gelatinous, greasy substance.

Through the occasionally open door could be heard the gentle bustle of an efficient hospital. This was clearly an outpost of the First World, almost like one of the hotels I stay in while traveling. But where, exactly? Everyone spoke excellent English, so Pakistan or India seemed a fair guess.

After the nappy change the nurses told me that it was also time to get my lotions topped up. Small tubes were inserted under the bandages that ran along my body. I then felt a chill creeping over my body, as a "restorative fluid" was pumped in through the tubes.

Lying quite still in a bed with sealed eyes and mouth is no way to spend a morning, but that is what I did. At least it gave me time to consider my position. I knew one half of the story; they knew the other half. I knew everything up to drifting at sea in the balloon basket. They knew how I had ended up here. At some point exchanges of information would be possible. I would need to be ready.

Information is the lifeblood of a successful life in sales. The single most important guiding rule is not to give anything away while at the same time squeezing out and sucking in as much information as possible yourself. Never stop asking questions.

Never ask questions that can be answered "yes" or "no." Try to answer all questions with a question. But never do any of these things if it might make you sound devious.

For example:

BUYER: Does this model have the flexibility required to satisfy my future expansion plans?

SALESMAN: What do you mean by flexibility?

Wrong – sounds devious.

SALESMAN: How concrete are your expansion plans? Can we discuss them now?

Right – open things up.

At this time I also considered the setup here. The whole hospital caboodle was probably being paid for through insurance. Either that or the munificence of one of the balloon sponsors – perhaps even Mackenzie Industries. That was a stimulating thought. Indeed, the more I considered it the more convinced I became that I was simply benefiting again from some of the profits that I had in fact earned for the company. Beside, I doubt that Mackenzie Industries would have been quite so happy footing the bill if they'd seen Anthony's lack of effort in sponsorship acknowledgment.

It was good to have this period for thought. Other people tend to fill up your life with all sorts of pointless talking, severely limiting the time that can be spent with yourself thinking things through, making plans. If at any point you are trapped by someone who looks like they may want to start talking to you, stay as still as possible, making no sudden noises or movements. Anything can start them.

Moreover, when people do exchange words, chitchat, have a conversation, they seldom say that which they would most like to. For every "Lovely day, isn't it?" offered in daily exchange, there is a "Hold me in your arms forever" burning for release.

Just then two people entered.

"Good morning, Anthony, can you hear me?"

The kindly doctor. I moaned.

"Anthony, I am Dr. Patel. I have been treating you since you were admitted. You're making good progress."

I said nothing. I thought, "Patel – India!"

"Anthony, we're going to open a slight hole in your mouth now, so that you can take in some food. Only liquids at this stage but I'm sure you'll feel better for it."

Saliva began to fill my mouth. I had not realized how much I wanted some liquid. Dr. Patel was discussing the size of the hole required with the nurse. They both drew close. There was a slight pressure around my lips, then abruptly a sudden inrush of air which took me quite by surprise. I heard myself breathing deeply through the new mouth hole, producing a monotone whistling sound.

"How's that then, Anthony?" Dr. Patel asked warmly, himself clearly pleased. I blew air out through the hole and they both laughed, delighted.

"Your parents will be here after lunch. Before then I would like you to take some of this high-protein drink we have prepared. Don't drink too quickly – swallow slowly."

A straw was pushed through into my mouth. Tentatively at first I sucked and was rewarded with a cool, thick liquid which circled my mouth before disappearing downwards. What a feast! I started to gulp ferociously and the straw was abruptly pulled from my mouth.

"Anthony! No rushing please!"

The straw was replaced and I drank at the required speed. The liquid was delicious; a light, citrus flavor, smooth but bulky. Towards the end I decided to play the game a bit, demonstrating my helplessness by deliberately burbling some back out through the hole. Sure enough a hand was quickly there to mop the front of my face.

"Steady now, Anthony. As I said, take your time. You're still weak."

I moaned in understanding.

"Now, Anthony, the relatively sudden intake of liquid will go through your body at speed. Could I ask that, when you get the urge, you make some noise to tell us that you need a visit to the bathroom? We'd like to try and get you off the nappies."

I grunted in acknowledgment. Then we all waited for my urge. Dr. Patel was right – almost before I knew it my bladder had swollen hugely. I pitched a moan to get them on the ball. Quickly the sheets were pulled back and my statue-like frame was swiveled out by doctor and nurse, then tipped to place my feet on the ground, and finally stood up with one person on either side supporting me. We then moved forward as a team, with me mostly dragging my legs for effect. I did feel a little lightheaded, actually. How long had it been? I was turned abruptly into the bathroom.

"OK, we're approaching the toilet itself," Dr. Patel informed me. "Don't worry. I'll take care of this for you."

Before I knew it I could hear my water emptying into the bowl, directed by Dr. Patel. I was then done up again, turned round and helped back towards the bed. We stopped just short.

"I'd like to see how much power you have in your legs, Anthony. We're going to let go of you momentarily. We'll be right beside you all the time so don't worry about falling down. Straight ahead of you, not more than three steps, is your bed. Can you reach it?"

Gradually I felt their arms being ever so cautiously removed. I stood alone. For a split-second I assessed for myself how much strength I had by shifting weight slightly from leg to leg. Having done so to my own satisfaction I collapsed forwards for theirs. I was not yet in a position to accept the possible consequences of a show of strength. Not enough was known. I had felt quite steady, though. Dr. Patel and the nurse caught me midway down.

"Wow! Perhaps a little too much to expect for day one," Dr. Patel comforted me as I was raised back into bed. I burbled in response.

"Anthony – I am sure that you will have many questions."

Dr. Patel had come back shortly after my dinner. "It is terrible really," he chortled comfortingly. "If I go away for a couple of days to a medical conference in Delhi or Geneva or Sydney, I come back and gather my family around me and immediately get them all to tell me what has happened, what everyone has been doing and so on." He sighed. "But you. You have been on a fantastic adventure, Anthony, and yet are unable to ask a single question about anything."

He moved up the bed towards me. "Let me tell you, Anthony. This will change." His tone now was one of quiet yet absolute authority.

"Before you know it you will be free and able to ask as many questions as you want. But until then it is important that you rest and recuperate. Your body has been severely weakened. But we have been using the very latest . . . eh . . . repair program. Designed by me personally. You will recover and you will continue with your life."

I moaned appreciatively.

"Now Anthony, it is important that you rest."

Dr. Patel patted me lightly on the arm and went quietly out.

He was right. I would continue with my life. It was only a matter of gaining the information that would allow me to make the right choices. Soon enough I would be back in the job, opening my briefcase, signing contracts, draining glasses.

23. The Deepening Pit

Mr. and Mrs. Hislop arrived shortly before lunch. They were thrilled to see me and in particular the new hole in my face mask. Dr. Patel updated them proudly on the progress that had been made. Then some more of the thick liquid was, somewhat theatrically I felt, brought in and the Hislops exalted at seeing me suck it all down.

"That's my boy," Mr. Hislop claimed softly.

"Oh, Anthony, we missed you so much!" sighed Mrs. Hislop.

I moaned to make them happy. Mrs. Hislop started to cry gain. Dr. Patel said that, all things being equal, it might be possible to cut a hole for my eyes tomorrow. This announcement caused me some alarm. I gave a sharp intake of breath, making a shrill whistling noise. Mr. Hislop was alarmed.

"Anthony, are you OK? Anthony?"

Dr. Patel moved quickly to play down the moment,

"It's nothing. Anthony is naturally excited at the prospect of seeing you both again. I hadn't told him about opening his eyes tomorrow. You're excited, aren't you?" And he tapped the bed close to my hip.

"There are so many people who want to talk to you, Anthony," Mr. Hislop stated, quite excited himself.

I moaned helplessly. I could imagine the circus that awaited. Journalists, photographers, embassy officials, faraway relatives, police.

"Emma-Jane is planning to come over as soon as she can," Mr. Hislop continued. The name seemed familiar. Who was she? My sister? My girlfriend?

"I think that's enough for today. Anthony must be quite tired now."

Mrs. Hislop continued weeping. I gave a mild groan. Dr. Patel gently but firmly encouraged the parents to leave. They said goodbye to me and shuffled off down the corridor.

Getting through the next day would be difficult. I was going to have to play this very skillfully. I tried desperately to recall the color of Anthony's eyes. I knew they weren't anything like blue or grey; I could only hope that they were vaguely similar to my own. Were they thin or wide? Were my own? I couldn't remember. How far apart were they? Had he not been a little cross-eyed? My mind flew here and there, trying to conjure Anthony Hislop's eyes. All I had was the distant look as he let go of the balloon rope and I drifted away. It was all out of my hands now. I had only my own eyes to work with.

I was fed three more times that day. Each time I felt a bit stronger, more able, though I did not let on about this to anyone. I continued to move slowly, ponderously, each action an effort; any movement lasting more than thirty seconds was followed by pronounced sighing. After going to the bathroom I always collapsed on the way back to the bed, having to be semi-carried to my resting place. In spite of this all the nurses remarked continually on the good progress their "little hero" was making. Again I could detect Dr. Patel's tutelage. I got hardly any sleep that night, possibly because I'd been dozing a good bit during the day. When I did sleep I dreamt of eyes.

The next morning I was still finishing my first milk drink when Dr. Patel came in and announced with majesty that it was time to let me see the world again. I could hear him pacing as I lingered over the last dregs. Eventually there was nothing left to suck and my bed was swiftly cleared of all breakfast material. Dr. Patel sat down on the covers next to me.

"Anthony, the skin on your eyes was not terribly burnt when you came in, so I am most confident that there will be little pain when we remove their covering. Perhaps some mild discomfort. Undoubtedly it will take some time for your eyes to become re-accustomed to the light. When I do cut out some holes I would like you to open your eyes gradually."

He got up off the bed and I heard him pulling the curtains shut. Then he sat down on the bed again.

"The room is now quite dark. But remember what I said. It's been two weeks since you last used your vision."

I gasped. Two weeks!

"Don't worry. Now please stay quite still. Do not react to any pressure around your eyes. Hold quite still."

He then placed on hand lightly on my forehead. I felt something touching just below my right eye, a slight pressure and then the most delicate cutting movement began as Dr. Patel traced a small circle around the socket.

"That's one," he said, relaxed, satisfied.

He then placed one forefinger on either eye at the top of the cut, then softly peeled each patch down. A quick tug at the bottom and my eyes had been cleared. I kept them tight shut.

"Please, Anthony; slowly open your eyes."

What was the rush? I wanted to scream. I wanted to run away. I wanted to be somewhere else. Slowly though, I began to raise my eyelids. As light gradually entered there was a mild discomfort, my eyes screwing up in reaction. The edges of my vision were still slightly obscured by the remaining facial pack. Nevertheless I was amazed at how quickly I was able to see around me. Everything cried out to be looked at. Dr. Patel was sitting on the end of my bed, grinning broadly – a happy-looking Indian chap in his mid-forties with a receding hairline. Well fed. He raised his hands, palms upwards, and gesticulated at the four walls around me. I looked around and could see that the walls were unevenly covered with something.

Consciously shifting focus I looked closer – newspaper cuttings. At this distance I could not make out the writing – only the odd large headline was legible: "BALLOON BOY VANISHES" was one; "UFO MYSTERY" another.

The white, rounded ends of my bandaged hands and feet were sticking out from under the sheets and I could just see that I had on a pair of blue and white striped pajamas.

"How is it, Anthony? Good?" Dr. Patel was up now, approaching me.

I moaned. Dr. Patel's bright happy eyes met mine. His white coat was immaculate. He was an immensely proud doctor.

"Jolly good! Jolly good!" he informed me, then reached into his pocket for a pair of dark sunglasses and placed these on me, securing them with a short piece of elastic round the back of my head. Thank goodness for that. Without another word he then bustled out the door, though not far down the corridor, returning in conversation with a man, carrying a metal case, who must have been waiting nearby. Was this Mr. Hislop? He did not appear as I had imagined him. No, this man was also Indian. He quickly extracted a camera with a large flashgun from the case which he then set up on a tripod he had had slung on his back. Dr. Patel then came and stood next to me, placing his arm portentously round my shoulder. There was an almighty flash and the world went white. I heard movement but it was several minutes before I was able to make anything out again. When the room did come back into focus, no one was there.

A nurse came in with another milk drink.

"Good morning, Anthony. You look much better today," she said, sticking the straw into my mouth. "You'll need lots of energy, now, yes?"

I didn't answer. I was thinking of the impending arrival of the parents. What if they came right up close and looked into my eyes like Dr. Patel had done?

I should of course have realized that Mr. and Mrs. Hislop would be every bit as nervous as me. They walked softly into the darkened room and stopped, outlined ominously in the doorway. With a loud sob Mrs. Hislop swooped to my side.

"Anthony! Oh Anthony! Your eyes!"

She looked at me and I looked at her. I could feel her desperation to hug me. For the first time I could see her, too. In Anthony's photograph she had seemed almost small. In the flesh she was so much more; a round-figured woman, with dark (too dark?) hair and happy red cheeks. She wore large, single-pearl earrings, like punctuation marks on either side of a big head. Her teeth were slightly yellow. A thick, white cotton cardigan was worn over a pink T-shirt embroidered with lilacs. There were tears in her eyes. She peered deeply into my sunglasses, trying to find something. I moaned, ill at ease with what was needed from me.

"Oh, son, I can remember your beautiful eyes so clearly. Dr. Patel says you must wear the sunglasses for a couple of days. Just to be sure, you know."

"Oh Anthony," Mr. Hislop said, "You and your ballooning!"

They both laughed and I moaned softly, making a light tune for them. Dr. Patel came over and produced a packet of paper tissues, offering them to Mrs. Hislop.

"For your own eyes."

Mrs. Hislop took them and dabbed gently at her sodden cheeks. Mr. Hislop looked on, content with this happy family moment.

Dr. Patel left us to attend to other patients and we then had lunch together. The Hislops dutifully ate some sort of sausage and potato dish, the sort of look-alike food served up to foreigners who refuse "foreign stuff." I sucked my milk in silence. It was no fun watching them chomping away on nice, solid food. After every third or fourth mouthful they would smile at me, Mr. Hislop sometimes winking playfully. After finishing he got up and went to get some tea.

Mrs. Hislop put her lunch onto the table and went over to her shoulder bag.

"Your father and I thought you might like some photographs, you know, from home. We brought these from your room."

She smiled.

"Oh Anthony, I know you don't like us going into your room but we felt you'd want these." She tentatively produced a series of photographs, which she held a mere foot from my face. The first was of Anthony and Mr. and Mrs. Hislop standing next to a big, four-door car outside a white church. As I was taking in this image, studying it for information, it was whipped away and replaced with that of a pretty blonde girl with a blue bow in her hair. It was a college or school photograph.

"I spoke to Emma-Jane not one hour ago. She's booked her seat. It's all very exciting for her. The *Accrington Observer* is paying for the flight. It's an exclusive or something."

I looked at the smiling face of Emma-Jane. She was about Anthony's age, large-eyed and a wide mouth. Attractive in a plain way. When she laughed she would be very attractive, I thought. Were I to meet her in a hotel lobby I would undoubtedly try to take her to dinner. A nice, opulent restaurant, where the emphasis is on the ceremony of the serving rather than the quality of the food, would be the ideal place. To bring joy to a plain girl's face – that is surely worth the price of a cheap meal.

Another photograph, of a black sheepdog. "Bobby misses you, too."

She placed the photograph down on the bed with the others. Mr. Hislop came back with two teas. I looked down at the photographs. They sipped their tea.

"Anthony," Mr. Hislop said tentatively, "We know things have been difficult for you. So don't push yourself too much. Emma-Jane has already postponed the wedding to give you time to make a full recovery."

I could not even moan. Straightforward misery was beyond me now. My head sank back into the pillow. I searched my mind for a quotation, some pithy saying or phrase, but found none. Most things are endurable if you have a fitting quotation. I looked back at Mr. and Mrs. Hislop. They were smiling.

I realized I had dozed off. Dr. Patel was tapping my shoulder with one finger. He must have sensed my alarm.

"Calm now, Anthony, it's only me. Your parents left a few hours ago. I think they must have tired you out, eh?" He chuckled quietly to himself.

I said nothing.

"I'd like to expand the hole for your mouth, to allow you to take some solid food. I'm sure this will be all right."

He was sitting on the bed now.

"And hopefully you might be able to manage a word or two as well, eh?"

Dr. Patel laughed again, then reached into his pocket for a scalpel in a sealed transparent cover. He ripped this off and leaned forward to my mouth.

"This will be just like your eyes. Keep absolutely still, please."

Dr. Patel began to score a series of horizontal lines from the central hole to my left cheek, before doing the same with the right. He removed the blade and sat back, inspecting his handiwork. Then he reached forward and picked off about ten thick tabs of bandage.

"Anthony, how's that? Try and say something."

"Gggrh," I managed, trying desperately to sound American.

He looked disappointed.

"Try a bit harder. The bandages and treatment fluid around your face may have hardened a bit but your mouth and cheek muscles ought to be able to crack this."

I tried again. Sure enough, as I did so I felt a strain and then a light breaking sensation as something within the mask gave way.

"Goodness me!" I said breathlessly, although my words were smothered flat by my, as yet, static mouth and cheeks.

Dr. Patel started clapping like a child.

"How do you feel? Does it feel good?" He leaned forward excitedly, eyes sparkling.

"Fine, thank you," I said softly, the facial constraints making this sound like "Ine Uk Yu." "Can I have a look in the mirror, please?" I asked.

He looked at me in absolute puzzlement. I repeated my request, emphasizing "mirror," which came out "Irir."

Dr. Patel clicked. "Of course, of course. Can you manage with me alone?"

I allowed myself to be supported by him initially, then collapsed dramatically backwards on to the bed. He beetled out of the room to get assistance.

I tried a few noises just to hear my own voice. "Oooh," "Aaah," "Waiter!" "A large one, thanks," "Put this on my bill, please." None of these sounded English, let alone convincing.

Dr. Patel the speechgiver reappeared with a nurse.

"Come along then, Anthony," he cajoled, as the nurse took the other side and we advanced as one into the bathroom.

The combined effect of the sunglasses with the letterbox mouth hole gave me the appearance of a thin, disappointed snowman. Very little of my lips showed at all. I asked to go back to bed. And again I tested the strength of my legs on the way back. There was no doubt that my body was recovering well. At the same time, though, I needed to understand fully what had happened and, more importantly, what they thought had happened.

"Dr. Patel," I called as he was about to leave the room. He came quickly over.

"Dr. Patel. I need to know what happened." After the third time he understood what I was saying.

"Of course you do, Anthony, of course you do."

He froze momentarily, thinking, then pulled up a chair next to the bed.

"Anthony. You must understand and forgive me for my . . . prudence. We have to take things slowly." He leaned over and placed a deliberately reassuring hand on my shoulder. "No one who has been through what you have would find it easy to come to terms with. As is often the case, the real damage may well be internal, you know, up here," and he tapped his forehead twice.

"How long was I at sea?" I asked. Then again. Then again.

"We have pieced together a pretty good idea of what you have been through. We had to in order to determine the best treatment. Some people might have given you the standard stuff. That fellow in Auckland. Or Van Hedring in Cape Town. Not me, though. I understand sun burns."

He stood up now, moving into a lecturing mode with which he was more at ease.

"You were last spotted by a British Airways 747 somewhere over Burma. You then disappeared completely and, to be perfectly frank, it was presumed by everyone concerned that you were dead.

"In this respect the last few weeks have been a particularly beastly time for your parents. First you are dead, then you are found, then you . . ." He stopped, clearly annoyed that the most difficult subject had been unintentionally broached, and looked at me, weighing the silence. "The next thing anybody knows, you turn up I the Bay of Bengal four weeks later bobbing along in the balloon basket. The Pakistani naval helicopter thought you were a Burmese refugee at first. It was all quite extraordinary!" and he clapped his hands in wonder, before settling on the end of the bed.

"You were taken to Chittagong, in Pakistan. Now the local doctor, just your average doctor, who first examined you could see that you were badly ravaged by the sun and he quickly covered your skin in a cooling cream he had for overexposed aid workers. Things really got moving when the police identified you from your overalls. Soon the pieces began to fall into place. You were the missing balloon person!"

Again, the clapping hands.

"It was at that point, and not a moment too soon, that I was first contacted by the authorities in Chittagong. They faxed me full details and asked my opinion. It's quite a thing for Pakistan to ask India for help, you know. We're not the best of neighbors. Nevertheless, as the foremost authority on exposure burns and other dermatological damage, they were anxious to have my prognosis. I realized immediately that, just considering the amount of time you must have been at sea, they had seriously, maybe fatally underestimated the damage you had sustained. I mean, four weeks at sea, exposed. That is really something. I flew immediately to Chittagong. In the meantime I ordered that you be fully covered in thick moisturizing cream from head to foot."

He smiled broadly, waiting, I think, for some type of thanks. When none was forthcoming he continued unperturbed.

"It was the least I could do. After all, there was a strong possibility that exceptional harm had already been done. You may have appeared to have only light to middling burns but the facts of your case stated otherwise. You could not possibly have floated for several weeks in the Bay of Bengal without sustaining much deeper skin tissue damage. Hence my prescription of long-term restorative treatment. I was able to persuade the authorities that it was here in Calcutta that the correct facilities were available for your rehabilitation. In the end it allowed the two governments to make some form of statement about "humanitarian concerns having no borders" and so forth. When I went to Chittagong I took along a large supply of my own skin-healing cream, which was applied forthwith. I then escorted you back here personally."

He paused again.

"And . . . eh . . . since then we have continued with the regime of specialist preparations, wrapping and rewrapping and so forth, for about a month now."

"So how badly damaged am I?" I asked with apparent and genuine nervousness. Three times.

Dr. Patel dropped conspicuously down into a well-studied "breaking the bad news" gear.

"Well, as I said, it is inconceivable that you could have avoided extreme damage with such prolonged exposure to direct sunlight, particularly at sea where the reflected rays make the situation doubly harmful. But I am very hopeful that the prompt application of fine treatment will have minimized all long-term damage."

I was truly frightened, whining involuntarily. "How bad will I look?" Just twice.

"Of that Anthony, we cannot yet be sure. Before your face was covered the skin was looking very worn, very tired and heavily creased, with severe swelling. This is just as we would have expected after an experience such as your own. We will not know until the bandages and cream are removed."

"When will that be?" I asked desperately.

"In about one week." Then I can be sure that the treatment will have done all that it can.'

One more week and then the game would be up the pole. Not to mention the scarring for life.

"I know what you're worrying about," Dr. Patel said in a low, caring voice. Somehow I don't think he did. He came and sat quite close to me, picking up one of the photographs from the bedside table. He held it lightly with both hands, in a studied "contemplative" pose.

"You're worried about Emma-Jane, aren't you?" He looked to me for confirmation.

I had to join in. Besides, it was also true. She would be here soon enough and could well figure me as not-Anthony immediately.

"Yes," I said softly.

"Love is a wonderful thing, Anthony. Its force and power can overcome the strongest of obstacles."

"Yes," I agreed softly.

"Anthony, I want you to be brave and strong."

He patted me on the shoulder. I was now whimpering.

"Now, Anthony, I cannot pretend that this will be easy for you. You do understand that, however bad the damage, this is merely the first stage towards recovery. If need be, there are all manner of avenues that can be explored. Cosmetic surgery and the like."

My God! What horrors had been worked on me?

Dr. Patel did not, of course, understand the total fear of my situation. A salesman needs a good face. Not a handsome or a beautiful one. But a good one. And it must be a comfortable face. One with which any of four key emotions can be quickly conjured.

First – Happiness. A salesman is always happy to see his customer. For example:

CUSTOMER: I wasn't expecting to see you creeping back round here again, not since you shafted me last time.

SALESMAN: It's great to be here again. And you look great too.

Second – Concern. A salesman is always concerned about every aspect of a customer's life. For example:

CUSTOMER: We'll have to be quick. The grandchildren are coming round in a moment.

SALESMAN: I won't delay you any more than is absolutely necessary. But I need to make sure that you're going to be able to take care of those grandchildren in the way that you really want to. Do you know what our latest model could do for your business?

Third – Surprise. A salesman is always surprised when something he has said isn't true.

CUSTOMER: My furnace exploded last week despite your assurance that it could withstand those temperatures.

SALESMAN: That is unbelievable. I will get onto our people immediately.

Fourth – Disappointment. A salesman is always disappointed to lose any business.

CUSTOMER: So while I'm giving a little bit of the order to your rival, 99% of it is yours. Shall we have a drink?

SALESMAN: I have to be honest – that "little bit" hurts. Can we talk about this?

Happiness – Concern – Surprise – Disappointment. Without a reliable portfolio of these four facial expressions – one is always wearing one of them – a salesman is finished.

I lay quite still, my mind wrestling with the strong possibility that I might never again make another sale of any kind.

Dr. Patel popped his head back round the door as he was leaving. "Your parents will be here tonight, Anthony. Remember – be brave," and he punched the air with a fist.

I spent two hours with Mr. and Mrs. Hislop, during which time we had dinner. I was now on a sort of baby food mixture which Mrs. Hislop was permitted to spoon-feed me. She was unable to contain herself.

"Oh Anthony, you look so much more, more . . . human now."

I gurgled appreciatively.

"That's my boy!" Mr. Hislop chimed in.

I was far from happy and it showed. Dr. Patel had obviously explained that I was now able to communicate at a basic level. The Hislops arrived with expectations of a little chitchat. I mustered "Hi Mom, Hi Dad," but the thought of disfigurement and the end of my salesman's life had gutted me of any enthusiasm for role-playing. After a few "yes" and "no" answers the melancholia overwhelmed me and I spoke no more. While Mr. Hislop managed to stick to the upbeat script that Dr. Patel had prescribed, Mrs. Hislop left in tears.

Later that night Dr. Patel came in and tried to talk with me. I feigned sleep and after a few minutes of silent observation from the end of the bed he left.

Lying in the dark I struggled to maintain control of my thoughts. At sea in the basket it had seemed that t my life was about to end. How much worse it now was to be confronted with the end of the reason for life itself. I could not exist without selling. The room, still and quiet, hammered home my decision. It is an oft-mentioned phrase that "It's a long way to fall from the top." More shocking still is to realize how far one can fall from the bottom.

24. DISCOVERY

Dr. Patel came in the next day with a nurse whom he immediately ordered to remove the mitten-like bandages around my left hand.

"The hands," he explained slowly, "are exposed from birth to the elements. As such, their skin and superstructure are a good deal tougher than those of the rest of the body. Therefore we should expect the least damage to the hands. Let us now see."

"Are you sure?" I asked timidly, but he was intent on ignoring me.

A minute later Dr. Patel help up my hand, holding it carefully in the center by his thumb and forefinger, turning it over slowly. He then asked me to wiggle each digit in turn, inspecting them carefully as I did so.

"Anthony – this is most encouraging. Apart from some minor scarring there is minimal damage. That Is not to say that there is no damage. Merely that it is minimal. How do you feel?"

I declined to answer and he continued.

"We will cover your fingers in some of my treatment lotion, Type Four I think, nurse, and then seal it in with some light gauze. This will allow the healing process to continue and at the same time give you free use of the hand. You'll be able to hold things and so forth. Isn't that an improvement?"

I mumbled something rude, feeling no reason to be in a better mood. Dr. Patel was not happy. "Now listen to me, Anthony. There is no use lying there feeling sorry for yourself. I have seen people with far worse damage than yours go on and lead full and interesting lives."

I said nothing. Meanwhile the nurse freed my right hand before covering both in a light, greasy lotion.

"Anthony, please," he continued softly, "think of your parents."

I had dinner with Mr. and Mrs. Hislop again that night. They were delighted to see my hands. I made as if playing the piano for effect. When Mr. Hislop went to get the teas Mrs. Hislop performed "This little piggy went to market" up and down my fingers repeatedly.

Dr. Patel was back promptly the next day. He came in and explained that he felt that it should be possible to remove the stiffer layers of bandage, that the skin would now be able to take the strain of bending. "This will allow you much freer movement, Anthony. Indeed, you should be able to walk a little bit."

As he said this an Indian television camera crew arrived. Dr. Patel greeted them happily in Punjabi or some other tongue. Within minutes a full-scale production was underway at the foot of my bed, with Dr. Patel playing the lead role as the knowledgeable, caring physician. After about one hour they left and were replaced by a team of nurses who wheeled in an elaborate pulley contraption. This was used to hoist me above the bed while the nurses labored to remove the bandages, padding and all manner of wrapping, of which I had previously been ignorant. I was then gently lowered. Dr. Patel was euphoric.

"This is magnificent, Anthony. I knew that my treatment was good but these results are unprecedented. You felt no pain, no?" he asked timidly.

"No." As indeed I hadn't.

"Excellent. Try moving around a bit."

A degree of self-control was necessary. I could feel that my limbs were strong and perfectly able and was myself eager to flex them. At the same time it was important to maintain the illusion of weakness, of things not being ready yet. If Dr. Patel had his way I'd soon be sitting down to a mammoth press conference. So instead of waving and kicking with delight, I simply flinched slightly, then broke down in mock tears. Quickly Dr. Patel ushered out the nurses and came to my side.

"Oh Anthony, please do not cry. Your salty tears might affect the facial ointment you have on."

I wailed all the more.

"Listen to me now," and I sensed impatience for the first time, "things are looking extremely good. Far better than could have been expected. My revolutionary new treatment is working wonders."

He got up to go, then paused. "To be honest, Anthony, I am beginning to wonder if it is not the case that most of your problems are up here," and he tapped my bandaged forehead reproachfully.

That night, when I was absolutely sure that everyone was asleep, I got up and walked around. As I had expected, neither standing nor walking was a problem. There was a small balcony behind the drawn curtains. Peeking out I estimated that this was the tenth floor or so. I then read all the newspaper cuttings but didn't find out anything new. Turning back to the bed, the chair that Dr. Patel always used stood on the left, to the right a bedside table with a lamp. On it were three photographs and a Get Well card with a picture of a cowboy from Mr. and Mrs. Hislop. Instinctively I looked under the bed and found a suitcase. It was one of those disgusting plastic and cloth tourist jobs, with white go-faster stripes laid onto the blue vinyl. I shuddered to think that so many nights had been spent near this terrible creation. Inside was an assortment of clothes, presumably Anthony's, including the requisite college sweat top and pants, together with a pair of black "smart" shoes and an old pair of trainers. I considered this before replacing the suitcase exactly as I had found it. Instinctively, I yanked open the small drawer in the bedside table. Nestling petitely alone was a Gideon Bible.

No traveler has ever received as much inspiration, taken such succor from it, as I did then, grabbing the text and kissing it passionately. That book was the first tangible reminder of my old life. All that was needed now was a hotel room to go around it. But more than anything else this discovery told me that I needed to take control. It was no use just waiting for things to happen to me. Active, I could move things in my favor; passive, it was only a matter of time before I was exposed. I walked around the room until I felt tired, slowly easing my limbs back into play. I had no idea what I would need to do yet, but being physically unready would not help. Pacing, my life seemed to be on track again. Where once I was lost, now I was found. Almost home.

25. Revelations

The next day my facial mask was cut along the jawline and a form of elasticated hinge inserted on either side. This made eating normal food possible and talking much easier. Now I was forced to approximate Anthony's accent, although this development had been anticipated. My memory of this voice from the rainforest was hazy but, having spent so much time listening to the banal chatter of Mr. and Mrs. Hislop, I was able to produce what I felt would be a convincing rendition. Importantly, my face was far from completely free as yet, allowing a significant margin of error.

"Gosh, Anthony – your voice sounds so deep," Mrs. Hislop said softly, somewhat taken aback. I explained that my throat was still a bit sore. Mr. Hislop told her to "leave it out, Marge! I'm just happy to be talking with my boy again," and he sandwiched my right hand between his two massive mitts. I was given the same lunch as them – sausages, chips and beans. "Just like you like them, son," Mrs. Hislop cackled.

Mr. and Mrs. Hislop were generally happy that day. They sat on either side of the bed, hands linked over my feet. Their eyes spoke of resurrection and redemption while my own feelings shouted violently of the chasm ahead. With each step towards apparent normality, I became increasingly uneasy. The freedom of my lusty, chewing jowls was in sharp contrast to the prison of circumstance being constructed by the hour. Sooner or later something would have to give.

"Anthony, how do you feel?" Mr. Hislop asked, smiling.

Performance time.

"I feel great, I feel just great."

"Oh son, oh my son," Mrs. Hislop whispered softly as she crumpled down on to the bed, Mr. Hislop leaning over to hold her.

"There, there, dear; there, there." He turned and looked at me, winking slyly. He kept doing this, presumably one of those tedious father-son bonding things. I nodded back and he smiled. Things were going well. Mrs. Hislop eventually stopped crying. Mr. Hislop said, "Anthony, you know, your voice does sound a bit different. I expect it's all that bandage and all," and he laughed lightly.

"Guess it must be so," I replied.

"You know, Anthony," Mrs. Hislop sniffled, "it's like you almost sound, well, English." They both chuckled at the thought. I joined in as best I could, making a note to enhance my accent. "Just wait till Emma-Jane hears you now," Mr. Hislop said. "She'll think she's marrying Prince Charles, not plain Anthony Hislop from Ohio!"

Mrs. Hislop rubbed my left toe affectionately. "She'll be here tomorrow, you know. Isn't that great?"

So soon.

"That was quick," I blurted. "Yes – it's brilliant news."

Not a wonderfully coherent response on reflection. Surely Dr. Patel must have told them that I'd had a terrible experience;

that I was still coming to terms with my failure in the balloon; that I was dazed, confused, and displaced; that I might be in a state of denial. Surely he would be telling them all these things and more. I moaned weakly, surprising both myself and Mr. and Mrs. Hislop. My resolve was slipping. Mr. Hislop peered forward anxiously.

"Anthony? Anthony, are you OK?"

Dr. Patel diagnosed over-exertion, combined with a degree of over-excitement caused by Emma-Jane's imminent arrival. Under the circumstances I was more than happy to accept the mild tranquilizer he administered. Yet even with these little pills my sleep that night was at best fitful. What type of person had I been to merit such punishments?

Breakfast was sweaty. I was drenched from ceaseless tossing and turning. About one hour later I heard a group of people coming down the corridor. They stopped just before reaching my room, allowing Dr. Patel his melodramatic last-minute reiteration of "the facts," something which preceded all visits. Suddenly, they were all there: Dr. Patel striding forwards across the room, followed by a diligent Mr. and Mrs. Hislop. And behind them, first peering round the door, then standing apprehensively in the doorway, then rushing headlong towards me, was Emma-Jane. Long, blonde hair flew behind her as she flung herself on her knees beside the bed, head nestling into my arm.

"Anthony! Oh, Anthony!" she gasped breathlessly. Mrs. Hislop was herself being supported by Mr. Hislop. Both were weeping with joy. Dr. Patel wiped his sleeve across his face. As my vision blurred I realized that I too had given myself up to the heady atmosphere. So there I sat, propped up in bed in some well-to-do Indian hospital or other, wrapped as a mummy, wearing sunglasses, with tears streaming down inside and over my bandages. On my left, the joyful fiancée of the balloon pilot I had marooned in the jungle, on my right his equally joyful parents, and with them the diligent doctor. I felt their presence burning its way into my very being.

It was, of course, inevitable that Emma-Jane and I would be left alone. Dr. Patel gave his apologies almost immediately, satisfied that the ringmaster role had been played out to the full. Mr. and Mrs. Hislop lingered. Their delight at seeing us together was unmistakable but soon they were making the smallest of talk. Throughout this period Emma-Jane said very little. She sat on the bed, cradling my left hand, occasionally glancing up at my face. She was plainly dressed but in a way which accentuated every aspect of her femininity. It was not vulgar – it was the simple display of a modest upbringing, where you learn to make do and to make the most. Her hair was styled without being choreographed. Emma-Jane was significantly more attractive than the dull photograph had implied.

All the time Mr. and Mrs. Hislop kept the chatter going. They explained what Emma-Jane had told them about the ongoing coverage of the story in Ohio. I wasn't just front-page news – I was the news. Prior to my being found a group of ex-classmates – "You remember Horsey Ed" – had banded together to raise money for a memorial statue. Even after I was discovered alive the city council was actively considering the possibility of an appropriate public honor. My heroism had apparently made everyone very proud to be from Accrington.

Still, for all the time these and other details of the waiting circus were being tutted and fretted over in jolly conspiratorial tones by Mr. and Mrs. Hislop, Emma-Jane said next to nothing. She sat on the bed, simply being with me. At first I could not understand this. Like everyone else in the room she must have been briefed by Dr. Patel on the likely nature of my injuries. What young woman would want such pain in her life? Scarred tissue, warped skin, permanent disfigurement – these were terrible things. Yet still she sat. And this was not the determined, stiff-upper-lip caring of someone who knows their time has come, who knows that they are "needed." No, this was the purest desire merely to be with someone else. It was love. Emma-Jane loved me with all her heart.

When a second silence had endured for an appreciable period, Mr. Hislop tugged softly on his wife's sleeve.

Come on, dear. I reckon these two young lovebirds have plenty to chat about without us."

With the mirthful mock nervousness of any parents they scuttled off down the corridor. We sat alone. In all this time barely a sentence had been exchanged directly between us. Emma-Jane looked up at me. I felt I needed to say something

"Hello." Laughing nervously.

She smiled. "Hi."

ME: "I've missed you."

EMMA-JANE: "I've missed you too."

ME: "How is everyone? Back home?"

EMMA-JANE: "They're fine. Everyone says hi!"

We both laughed.

EMMA-JANE: "Do you have any condoms?"

I was about to ask what for when the truth nailed me. Surely not?

"What's wrong, Little Anthony? Cat got your tongue?" She smiled sweetly and I felt her hand moving slowly but firmly over my body and under the top sheet. This was not what I had expected.

"Emma-Jane – listen . . .you have to stop."

"Anthony – come on. Don't you want to play?"

"Yes – oh yes, it's just that . . ."

"Don't worry – I had a private word with Dr. Patel. There's no damage down here."

She poked playfully at my crotch, continuing, "And I for one do have condoms."

She reached behind into the back pocket of her blue jeans and plucked out a lurid red condom pack, placing it on the bed with a triumphant "Ta-da!" She then went to the door, checked the corridor, slipped the catch on and twisted the Venetian blind to the closed position. Then back to the bed. Or rather, on to it. From about four feet she leapt, landing with amazing grace and poise astride my trembling body. Slowly she leaned forwards and kissed my bandaged forehead, then down to my mouth hole, which she also kissed before forcing the tip of her tongue through.

"Oh Anthony, my little tractor driver, I've missed you."

Throughout she was grinding her crotch with vigor down into mine. I was feeling faint, mumbling, "No no, no . . . mmh."

"Yes!" she murmured. In a furious whirl of white my sheets were ripped off, her pants removed and a hand was raking feverishly through the bandages, creating the necessary outlet. And then – shocked, dazed, traumatized – the condom was on me and I was inside her. Had I not been agnostic I knew I would be going straight to hell for this. Yet for those few moments my feelings were of complete, wondrous, magnificent elation.

Emma-Jane left shortly thereafter. Dr. Patel had given her a strict time limit and she did not wish to jeopardize future visits. She kissed me, gave a gloriously lascivious smile, and said that she'd be back tomorrow.

I spent the evening in contemplative mode. My basic thought was – why couldn't I be Anthony Hislop? Mr. and Mrs. Hislop needed and wanted a son. Sweet Emma-Jane needed and wanted a husband. There was no good reason why I could not fulfill on both counts. Indeed I was already playing the role. Beside, and make no mistake about it, my career as a top international salesman of machine tools was probably over. The awful damage wrought to my face would put an end to that. Therefore I needed a new career and being Anthony Hislop seemed as good as any. Coping with my disfigurement would be a period of great trauma. I would need the support of a nice family unit. This was the answer to all our problems.

The door snapped sharply open. Dr. Patel came in, effusive.

"Anthony, Anthony – good morning!"

"Good morning, Dr. Patel, how are you?"

"No, no, Anthony – how are you?" He sat on the end of the bed, waiting for my response. Then he got up and strode excitedly up to the window, looking down like a benign god on the world below. He turned, still waiting for my answer.

"Fine," I choked out. "I think."

"Good. Excellent," he said, approaching the bed, stopping at the foot. His face showed total, unadulterated commitment.

"Anthony – I am entirely satisfied with our progress to date. My treatment is exceeding even my own expectations. Tomorrow we will remove your facial bandages."

He slapped the bed with joy; the vibrations, the waves which now threatened to wash over me.

"Is this wise?" I asked nervously.

"Under normal circumstances, Anthony, the patient is more eager than anyone to have his or her bandages removed. Your apparent reluctance, despite the promising results so far, indicate that there is a psychological barrier."

"What do you mean?" I was suspicious.

"It means that part of you is scared, terrified of moving forward. This is quite common in injuries of this type. The victim prefers the security of the hospital and being a patient to getting out and rejoining life. Your minor problem yesterday, and somewhat recalcitrant attitude in general, fits entirely with this diagnosis."

"I see," I said softly.

"Do you see, Anthony? Do you? If you do you will understand how important it is that we do not pander to this backward drive. Sometimes it is necessary to force people to be free."

"Of course." I nodded slowly.

"That is not to say that we must throw all caution to the wind. We will proceed with care. All your body treatments will be removed tomorrow morning. This will allow us to make a more informed judgment about whether or not it is wise to proceed with your face. But if your body as made appropriate progress, and I have every reason to think that it has, then the face will be uncovered as well."

"Will Emma-Jane be there?" I asked earnestly.

"That is a good example of applying unnecessary pressure. All the work will be completed while you are alone. Then your parents and then Emma-Jane will join us. They have agreed to this schedule. It is a sensible step-by-step approach. Our aim is to make strong, gradual progress."

"Thank you, Dr. Patel," I said unenthusiastically. He didn't notice.

"Not at all, Anthony, not at all. You know I only have your interests at heart. That is what matters most: what is right for you."

Dr. Patel patted me on the shoulder and left. Listlessly looking around the room, I noticed that he had left behind a couple of folders. I hastily got up to take a peak. One contained an extensive medical history of the recovery program, detailing the various treatments used. The other contained several faxes and contract proposals. One from *Time* magazine offered Dr. Patel $50,000 for the compete story of my rehabilitation. Another from the *National Enquirer* confirmed that they would pay $100,000 for a story called 'LIZARD FACE BALLOON BOY – ASTONISHING INSIDE MEDICAL STORY." There was a large red tick on this one.

26. REPTILE

I woke up with a start the next day after a weary night of attempted sleep. Again and again I had crashed my head down into the pillow, hoping of some relief. But a few minutes later would find me pacing the room, my mind full of the shocked faces of Mr. and Mrs. Hislop when the bandages were cut and they were presented with their LIZARD BOY son. And what of me? I did not wish to continue life as a reptile. The dark had worked away at my positive thoughts of a happy new life in rural America. Getting through these next few hours was all that I could think of now.

Dr. Patel came into the room followed by two nurses and a hospital orderly with a trolley that was placed next to the bed. On it were an assortment of colored fluids, two tubes of cream and some cotton wool.

The pajamas were carefully removed and I was laid flat on the bed. One nurse stood on either side and began to unwrap each arm. Each time I lifted my head to observe I was told to "please lie down, relax." The arms were finally naked and Dr. Patel inspected them. With an abrupt wave of the hand he pronounced himself satisfied and went to stand at the window while my legs and torso were competed. These too were considered and passed. Without so much as a word I was shoved back into the pajamas. Dr. Patel sent the two nurses away and positioned himself at the end of the bed.

"There is no doubt in my mind that we should now proceed with your face. The indications from the rest of your body are . . . sufficient." He looked at me, searching for dissent.

Suddenly the door swung open and the two nurses came back in with another similarly equipped trolley. There was also a bib which one of the nurses immediately tied around my neck. Dr. Patel moved round to the trolley and then looked at me like a proud father. "Time to be free," he announced importantly. I was asked to close my eyes and the sunglasses were removed. After thirty seconds or so the instruction came to open my eyes. This I did, blinking frantically. Dr. Patel had me follow the mini-torch light again, then pronounced himself happy.

He picked up a scalpel and cut lightly at the back of my head, taking a pair of pointed scissors and pushing them gently into the opening, cutting upwards. After a good bit of pushing like this the scissors were removed and I felt fingertips working to free something. Then before my eyes passed Dr. Patel's hand, holding one end of a length of bandage. Again and again his hand appeared before my face as the strip of linen was unraveled. Blood rushed to my head as the pressure was gradually released. And with each pass of the doctor's hand I felt the revolving door of my undoing spin faster and faster toward that moment when I would be spat out on to the grim doorstep of reality.

The turning ceased. My head stopped spinning. I was able to focus. At the end of my bed stood Dr. Patel flanked on either side by a nurse. The nurses were impassive while Dr. Patel smiled, but only with his lips.

"Anthony. How do you feel now?"

"A bit lightheaded," I said quietly.

"It will feel a bit strange at first. Rather like having had a motorcycle helmet on for a long time. Soon enough we'll give you a shave. For the moment though, I think a wash will suffice." He smiled again, then addressed me more sternly.

"Anthony, on no account touch your face. The healing process is still proceeding. Do not touch your face. Remember, in many ways this is just the beginning."

The nurses set about cleaning me now with warm water and various fluids on the trolley. Their gentle dabbing gave the distinct impression that they were most concerned about the state of my skin. My scalp felt incredibly itchy and I told Dr. Patel this. He said that the nurses would perform a bed hair-wash.

"When will my parents be here?" I asked apprehensively as hand after hand swabbed at my face.

"Soon enough, soon enough. Now take things easy. We've plenty of time to get your hair scrubbed clean," he concluded. One of the nurses went out and came back with two buckets of water on a trolley. I was helped to turn round – something I was more than capable of doing myself – across the bed with my head and shoulder sticking out over the trolley. One of the nurses then wet my hair using a sponge and continued to do so for several minutes. All this time Dr. Patel was explaining things to me.

"Anthony, your parents are well prepared for this meeting. They are aware of the effect that such a prolonged period in the sun will have on a person's skin, particularly the facial area."

These words alarmed me through earfuls of water. What on earth had happened to me? What horrors had Apollo's bright rays wrought in my flesh? Meanwhile the nurses washed on, their fingers delicately moving over my scalp.

"It is essential that you keep everything in perspective. Remember that your parents are going through a lot, too. You must help them as much as they will help you." What hideous creature had I become?

"Dr. Patel, can I see myself before my parents arrive?"

Dr. Patel did not answer immediately. I could hear him pacing the room, though not nervously. The nurses were now easing the suds out of my hair, squeezing harder but with consummate sensitivity.

"Anthony, I was hoping that you were not going to raise that point right now. I do not think it good that you see yourself right now. It has to be a gradual item."

I was unhappy with this.

"Doctor, I can't meet my parents without seeing myself first! I just can't!"

His reason for wanting this was now made clear.

"Anthony, don't you think that it might be better to experience your parents' comfort with your status, before you experience that condition yourself?"

I told him no. I told him I wanted to see myself first. Dr. Patel persisted. He had been here before. He understood the psychological importance of completing the program in the right order.

"Anthony. You must think of yourself in the third person. Try to imagine your own mind. Don't you think you should protect it was much as you can? Please understand what is in your own good. When you see for yourself how comfortable your own parents are with your present condition you will be much better prepared. Please, Anthony, think of yourself!"

His concern for me was touching. The nurses applied what was to be the second and final rinse. My mind was made up, though, and I became quite intense.

"Look, Dr. Patel. I know what I want. I want to see myself before my parents arrive. Now please can I have a mirror!"

I was firm but quiet and Dr. Patel recognized the threat.

"Fine, Anthony, fine. We'll get you a mirror."

My hair was being toweled dry now and I faintly heard the doctor tetchily stomping out of the room.

27. True Colors

I must have been sitting in a sort of stupor. Dr. Patel came back in with a briefcase-sized mirror under his arm. This brought me back to life. And it was only then that a bolt of terror struck me, as if from heaven. He approached and placed the mirror on the trolley besides the bed. I could not see into it properly and leaned forwards to do so. In a single deft movement Dr. Patel placed himself between me and the mirror.

"Now listen to me, Anthony. Your tissues have been damaged but it is not necessarily permanent. Your face is also, mmh, tired – from a severe ordeal. I can guarantee that further improvement is likely, particularly with the course of treatment I have in mind."

He ran out of breath and paused. I needed to know and this was no time for niceties.

"Step aside, Patel."

The doctor moved quickly to the left as if on coasters. I caught a first shadowy glimpse of the outline of a head, my head, in the mirror. I recoiled slightly, then gathered myself afresh. Leaning towards the mirror I saw the beginning of a forehead and then in a headlong rush, I was there. My goodness — it was magnificent! A halo appeared around my head which at first obscured the facial features. This I realized was the light from the window over my shoulder. Still, it was a pleasing effect. The face now before me was my own but it seemed so different from how I remembered it. I had a beard but my mouth, nose, cheeks – everything seemed to have thinned considerably. The whole effect was like meeting a distant but well-treasured cousin long thought dead. I looked more well-defined that I could ever remember being. And there was no scarring whatsoever. Far from it – my cheeks appeared as soft and lovely as the rounded four-star pillowcases on which they had so often come to rest after a taxing day. I noticed that my mouth was gaping slightly and shut it. Then opened it – then shut it. Fantastic. What jowls, and even through the beard I could see nice red lips. I leaned into the mirror now, pulling my lips down with my finger. Abruptly they were pulled from my mouth by Dr. Patel.

"Anthony! Please! You must take care. You can see for yourself how damaged your face is – do not tempt the fates by tugging and poking."

I stared at him in absolute disbelief. How could he say that? Could he not see the change in me? I looked at him quite speechless.

"Anthony – do not cry. It will only make you want to wipe your face. Be brave. Remember – you are still young."

I saw then what he saw. That I was a 21-year-old American boy. I turned to the mirror again and looked at the face of a middle-aged businessman, perhaps recently returned from a tropical holiday. There were the bags under the eyes from promised yet uncommitted orders; the wrinkles from waking for an early flight after only two hours' sleep; the looseness from a lack of exercise apart from smiling at customers; the hollow eyes from dreams long forgotten, swapped for the busy distraction of constant travel.

I came aware that my mouth was now a broad toothy grin. In every respect I looked delighted, thrilled. But I quickly realized that I needed to show some of the reactions that Dr. Patel had been expecting. With tremendous effort I forced down the corners of my mouth, narrowed my eyes, then turned slowly to display these sad features.

"Now, remember all that I have said. Think of your facial troubles as footsteps in the sand that can be washed away in time."

He had clearly been saving that one. Without hesitation a loud, anguished wail rose from my lips, filling the room with misery. He reacted sternly, altogether differently from what I expected.

"Anthony, I warned you. We have done as you wished. Had we followed my plan your parents would have been able to supply courage and support to you. Now the positions are quite reversed. You must show strength to them. Now you must help them cope."

I tried to lay it on thicker still, delving deep into my past for suitable inspiration. The only major disappointments I could find as a source were those involving early closing times for bars. This proved sufficient and my eyes were soon welling with water. Dr. Patel relinquished immediately his tough but caring medical professional act and grasped me firmly in his arms, repeating that most healing of all English phrases, "There, there." The nurses came back in, Dr. Patel released me and asked me to get back into bed properly. I said that I needed to go to the bathroom and they helped me in, withdrawing once I indicated the need to sit down. The door was not quite closed but after I was sure that they had moved a good few feet away I leapt up to examine my face again in the wall mirror.

Such fine features. Stepping back from the mirror I noticed something else – the rest of my body appeared thinner too. I climbed on to the toilet seat and pulled up my pajama top. Framed opposite was one of the most beautiful stomachs I had ever seen – and it was mine. I rubbed it feverishly. What a transformation.

"Anthony – is there anything wrong?"

Dr. Patel was calling me, anxious for my safe return. I gave my lovely stomach one last pat before presenting myself at the bathroom door, holding on to the doorframe, swaying slightly. The nurses dutifully helped me back into bed where I sat looking woeful and despondent. This was what was expected of me. Dr. Patel came round to the side of the bed again.

"I am going to fetch your parents. It is now your turn to show support for them. Together we can build your future, your life."

Dr. Patel and the Hislops had been outside the door for several minutes. I had heard them approaching and sat up properly for their entry. Dr. Patel's voice alone could be heard and I presumed he was warning them, preparing them for this encounter with their hideously disfigured son, reminding them of the importance of certain behaviors, explaining to them what they must and must not do.

The door moved slightly as someone took the handle, then swung wide open with bravado. Mr. and Mrs. Hislop trooped into the room wearing the type of rigid smile common to royal visits. Dr. Patel brought up the rear. They stopped at the foot of the bed and turned mechanically to face me, smiling all the while. Together, Mr. and Mrs. Hislop regarded me without necessarily seeing me. And froze in this tableau. Finally, I stepped into the silence.

"Mother! Father! How do I look?"

Things moved very quickly then. Mrs. Hislop's lip started to quiver violently and I gathered she was having trouble replying.

"Hello d-d-d-d," and then she collapsed on to the floor as if hit heavily from behind. Mr. Hislop dived to her side and I was left staring at the figure of Dr. Patel, who was shaking his head sadly. He then ran to the door and shouted for a wheelchair.

Five minutes later we were reconvened. Mrs. Hislop was sitting in the wheelchair, having been sedated by Dr. Patel. Mr. Hislop, no longer forcing a smile, was in a chair beside his wife, his hand on her knee.

"You look good Anthony, all things considered," Mr. Hislop said meekly, now smiling slightly. "How do you feel? It must be good to get that mask thing off."

I appreciated his interest.

"It sure is, Father. I feel so much better now. It's like a new world," I said, trying to be of use to him.

"Monster, monster," Mrs. Hislop mumbled. Dr. Patel had one of the nurses stand between Mrs. Hislop and me. Nevertheless, while her semi-prostrate figure was no longer visible, I kept hearing the odd phrase, racked with horror. Had I been her son I would have been most distressed. As it was, my suffering was merely the insult of being thought hideously disfigured when in truth looking better than I had for a couple of decades.

"Son, you know we'll care for you and Dr. Patel here says that we can expect improvement," Mr. Hislop said sternly, like a general addressing his army.

"I know, Father. For the moment I am happy just to be with you again," I said softly. Although Mr. Hislop held himself proudly, I suspected that tears were imminent. He controlled himself, though, swallowing the urge to be less than the strong figure he wanted me to see. I smiled at him and Dr. Patel, who was himself looking somewhat starry-eyed. They smiled back. In the darkened room we made a triangle of resolve, of determination. Mrs. Hislop, wife and mother, sketched a drugged backdrop of whispers and curses, allowing us to bask fully in the air of battle. Eventually they all left. As Mr. Hislop pushed his drugged wife along the corridor I heard him say, "I didn't think it would make his eyes so beady."

174

I was rather shaken by all this. Dr. Patel came back in and I asked for a glass of water. He sat on the bed and patted me manfully on the shoulder.

"Well done, Anthony, well done. How do you feel?"

"Fine, I guess."

"Good, that is good. Now, do not be overly concerned about your parents' initial reaction. That was only to be expected."

"How is my mother?"

"Oh, she is fine, she will be fine. You father is a very strong man. Both your parents are exceptionally proud of you. In time everything will be healed."

We sat quietly for a moment before Dr. Patel decided it was time to get back to business.

"Emma-Jane will be here in about two hours."

Of course! Sweet Emma-Jane. This reminder made me smile.

"She loves you very much, Anthony."

"I know, I know, and I love her."

"I am sure that everything is going to be fine. But you must be prepared to help Emma-Jane too if necessary."

I nodded slowly, grimly accepting the responsibility. It was the very least I could do for the girl who loved me so very much. Dr. Patel then adopted a more brisk tone.

"Now, as part of your rehabilitation program it is important that you familiarize yourself with all the various stories and reports that have been written about you. Part of the problem," he paused, "the psychological problem," and he tapped his forehead, "comes from the fact that you don't know who you are, who you have become." With that he went over and picked up a briefcase by the door.

"In here is a comprehensive package of newspaper and magazine cuttings from around the world. The vast majority are in English although we've included the odd foreign language one just to give a flavor of how big, how international, the story, your story, is."

He smiled broadly and unlocked the briefcase, taking out a one-inch-thick A4 file with the words "ANTHONY HISLOP – BALLOON" on the blue cover.

"This will give you something positive to do while waiting for Emma-Jane. You won't be able to get through it all today but it'll be a start."

"Thank you very much, Dr. Patel," I said appreciatively.

"Not at all, Anthony. Oh, here is one of today's papers, actually. There's an amusing impostor story on page three. You'll just have to get used to this sort of thing. It's the price of fame." He passed me a copy of the *International Herald Tribune*. "I'll pop back in before Emma-Jane gets here."

Dr. Patel departed with an avuncular handshake. I considered the cuttings in front of me, picking up the *Herald Tribune*. Page three, he had said.

BALLOON BOY – MYSTERY IMPOSTOR

Authorities in Bangkok are trying to establish the identity of an unknown man who was found wandering naked in the Thai rainforest. The man, who appears to be American, was found two days ago by a logging team near the town of Ko Man Say. He claims to be the balloon pilot Antony Hislop, who was himself found six weeks ago floating in the Indian Ocean. A US

Embassy spokeswoman said that every effort was being made to identify the young man, who was most likely the victim of a drug overdose.

My heart stopped. Then restarted, thumping wildly against my chest. The world about me was crumbling. I jumped out of the bed and stalked the room, mind racing. I caught sight of the bedside table drawer and pulled it and yanked out the Gideon Bible, my only link to real life. Yes! Get back to your own life!

I reached under the bed and heaved out the suitcase. I was leaving, and leaving now. The first priority was clothes. To be found wandering the streets of Calcutta in regulation hospital pajamas would be a decidedly inauspicious ending. I stripped and pulled on a pair of boxer shorts, a white T-shirt and a pair of white socks. Neither the jeans nor the chinos fitted. Ridiculously, I would have to make my escape in a pair of tight towelling trousers. I pulled the university sweatshirt on, too. At least bottom and top matched. And it would have to be the running shoes. Having established an outfit, it was time to sow some confusion, leave a couple of red herrings. All the while I listened closely for approaching footsteps. My only solace came from the fact that, having played incapacitated so well, no one would think that I had the energy to make a dash for it.

For starters I hid the pajamas, jeans, chinos and a couple of pullovers under the mattress, pushing the suitcase back under the bed. This way it would not be clear what I was wearing. Then I opened the window on to the balcony. Valuable time would be spent making sure I hadn't climbed onto the roof or whatever. Finally I picked up the photographs. On the back of each I wrote a different message in block capitals; first, "SEE YOU IN BUENOS AIRES," then "HELP – I MUST GO BACK TO THE SEA," finally "STARS ARE CALLING ME." I scattered these on the bed, then moved to the window and looked down onto the well-kept front lawn of a private hospital, considering my options.

The front way was impossible – far too many people. I walked to the door and listened. In the distance, the sounds of a hospital at work, up close very little. I slowly turned the handle and pulled the door open just enough to get an eye down the corridor. There was a reception desk at the far end. The lights leading up to it were off; everything was relatively dark. At the desk sat one male nurse reading a book. Good – a comedy. People reading tragedies and the like are more likely to look up, pained at some injustice or other.

I eased myself out of the door and, with my back firmly against the wall, slunk away from the light of the reception. There was a corner about fifteen feet away, which I stealthily attained. Ahead was a door set into the facing wall. Approaching closer, I made out the glorious words "Fire Escape." I tiptoed hastily towards it, my hand soon on the long bar that opened the door. With a final check over my shoulder I pressed down and pushed. There was a rush of wind, I stepped out into bright sunlight on a wrought-iron staircase, and behind me the inhuman scream of an alarm announced the breaking of a seal I had not seen. With every nerve electrified I pushed the door quickly shut, then began to leap down the stairs. As each floor landing approached I expected at any moment to run into the arms of a fleeing doctor, nurse or more mobile patient. And all the while, as I bounded two or three steps at a time down the vibrating structure, my feet banging down like cymbals, the strident siren called to the world. Down, down I sped.

It was not until the fifth-floor landing that I dimly heard the approach of footsteps to the fire door as I flew breathlessly past. Sure enough, at the midway point to the fourth floor, the door on the fifth shot open and the screams of panicking patients and medical staff were sucked into my wake. At the third-floor landing the door opened abruptly in my path. I had no choice but to close it, shoulder-charging it shut with my momentum. Nothing can defeat a salesman with momentum. From behind the door came cries of "Mercy, mercy!" while above me the clattering noise of terrified invalids and terrified, caring staff filled the air. On the second floor I met my moment. There was but one step to go before the landing would be cleared. With a bang the door behind me exploded outwards. Glancing round I saw a prone body on a trolley rocketing to freedom. It took me directly in the midriff and I was hurled backwards and over the metal railings. I looked back into the alarmed face of a nurse gripping what was now an empty trolley as I arced downwards. I turned, flailing, and saw that I was traveling with the body beneath me. We hit the ground together, my impact nicely cushioned. Behind me the pandemonium continued, yet before the first escapers reached the ground I was up and crashing through the rhododendron bushes that made for rather an attractive garden.

After about two hundred yards of flowers, bushes and assorted ornamental arrangements there was a man-sized stone wall which I scrambled up and over. Behind me the cacophony of sirens and screams went on and on. Then another wall, this time with barbed wire suspended on the outer side which I had to jump over, clattering down on all fours as I landed. I was now in a dark lane, with some very nasty-looking buildings in it. Some were wooden, some brick. None were desirable places to pass, let alone enter. A gruesome collection of inhuman hovels. The place reeked of humid decay. I turned and looked back at the wall. A large sign said in English "No Entry – Private – Guard Dogs," along with scribblings in other languages.

I ran along in the dirt for about five minutes or so before encountering another wall. It cut off my path, coming out at right angles from that surrounding the hospital. I was none too keen on what I had found outside the confines of the hospital. The wall represented an opportunity to get back inside somewhere. I scurried over it and found myself in a garden even nicer than that of the hospital. The bushes were even better cared for; more sparing in foliage with brighter flowers. Not too far in, I could discern a path. Walking slowly, it turned out to be a nice path, edged with well-chosen stones and not as dusty as might be expected. Someone took very good care of it. There wasn't a dead or dying leaf to be seen. Footsteps behind me, approaching quickly. I turned and saw myself approaching, or someone very like me. A middle-aged jogger in sweat pants and T-shirt, puffing heavily. I raised my hand in acknowledgment. He slowed, smiling.

"Hi, how are you doing, pal?"

An American, I deduced. He continued, "I tell you – it's not the heat that gets me, it's the humidity! Right?"

I smiled; he laughed heartily at his own good humor and was on his way, heavy steps thudding down the path. I became excited. I knew this type of person. I knew I could not be far from home. I started to walk in the same direction as my jogging friend. Two security guards, Indians, sauntered past, nodding politely to me. I nodded back, mopping my brow. They glanced in the direction of the wall and the distant sirens. Oh yes, what had I done when I climbed that wall – I had not dreamed of finding this. My pace quickened and soon I found myself jogging, too. More footsteps behind me. I slowed slightly to speed up the moment of contact. A large male figure went past, resplendent in white running vest and electric blue shorts. He held up his hand in greeting. That man is a serious runner, I thought, as his effortless strides took him past me and out of sight. I continued with my own frugal steps, amazed nevertheless at my energy. Jogging was a startling enough activity to find myself performing, and the wonder of my undoubted destination added a degree of excitement that was difficult to contain.

The path was curving. I felt myself drawing round to a center. I passed an ornamental pool at which sat a young man reading a letter, airmail envelope beside him on the bench. I could see that it was not a long letter – a few lines on a white sheet.

"Good day to you!" I called, but he did not look up. Running by, I caught the end of the note, although I had to lean a bit to do so. "I will always love you," in a female hand. "Plenty more in the sea, matey," I called over my shoulder in consolation.

I was drawn on as if in a vortex. Pad, pad, pad, pad – my feet on the path. It was a beautiful garden, with beautiful smells. Abruptly I was in the open and I came to a dead stop. Before me was one of the most magnificent hotels I had ever seen. Perhaps my judgment was a little clouded by circumstance but there was no doubting that it was a great hotel. I had known it would be a good hotel simply from some of the garden details. In particular the isolated pool with bench is a feature not found in any but the best hotels.

To my left was a lovely kidney-shaped swimming pool. It is this asymmetrical option which finds favor in those hotels which truly understand the complexities of modern business. Very few architects appear to understand that a square or oval pool offers less in the way of exploration than a kidney-shaped one. At the end of a hard day, it is not enough to swim mindlessly from end to end. No, the demands of modern business mean that it is in the irregular contours that the tense fevers of the day can be gently exorcised. I have never done this myself but I have watched it happen.

To my right was a patio arrangement where a couple of guests were enjoying what looked like a pot of tea. There were about fourteen empty tables and a waiter standing diligently by the door. Another jogger swept past me and I watched him sit down at one of the tables and take his pulse, holding his right forefinger to his left wrist while glancing occasionally at a yellow sports watch. I looked up at the hotel. Twenty-four, no, twenty-five stories of absolute familiarity. I had stayed on every floor possible. I had even stayed in the Bridal Suite more than once due to mix-ups and the like. I knew that everything I could need or desire lay within. My absence of credentials was neither here nor there; I knew how to behave. Thinking all this over, I walked up and down slowly, exhaling and inhaling deeply, stretching my leg muscles occasionally, as I had seen others do after completing a jog.

I felt sure that the seventh floor was a safe bet. This was never the floor of conference rooms or restaurants or business facilities. After that it didn't matter. Twin, double or single; I could be at home in any of them. Pacing the ground, I wondered if I was visible from reception. It was difficult to tell, looking in through the darkened entrance. I had to presume that I was. I decided to establish myself with a seat on the patio, near but not next to the most recently returned jogger. The waiter bustled over to me as soon as I sat down. I waved him away nonchalantly. the jogger and I exchanged weary smiles.

"What a heat," he said.

I nodded. "Don't get much hotter."

We nodded ourselves back into isolation. I waited until he decided to go back into the hotel, then followed about ten yards after him. When I got to the doorway I could see the reception quite clearly. Two women sat behind a huge mahogany counter. One got up to greet the returning jogger. The other stared at me, eager to do her duty. I stopped and asked the waiter the time, displaying my familiarity with the staff. I then moved to the reception, smiling.

"Good afternoon, sir. Did you enjoy your run?" she asked politely.

"Yes, thank you, just what I needed, actually. I'll be glad of a shower though," and I laughed merrily. As did she. Pause. Time for guessing.

"Room 724, please."

She turned and went to the key boxes. Stopping, she turned puzzled.

"Don't you have the key already sir? Did you definitely hand it in when you went out?"

It did not matter now. I could see that the boxes either side of her outstretched hand did have keys in them, so the next step was easy.

"Sorry, 723 – I keep forgetting."

Her hand reached up and pulled out a key. She came back and handed me both.

"There you are, Mr. McMurry."

I thanked her warmly and moved in the direction of the lift, shaking my head in mock post-exertion.

It was a manned lift. The operator was a tall juvenile, first job and nervous. "Where, which floor, sir?" he asked, hands gripped tightly.

"Seven," I said with confidence. I asked him how long he had been working here. Three days. Was he enjoying it? Yes. What were his ambitions? To save enough money to go to college. That's a good ambition, I told him. Where did his family live? Bombay. How was he liking Calcutta? It was different. Did he have a girlfriend? Oh no. What was the best restaurant in Calcutta? The Imperial Mess.

My floor arrived and I said thanks, goodbye. The ride and questions had taken about fifteen seconds and I had had to talk quickly, often cutting off his answers. I had, though, succeeded in building a vital bridge to him; questions about a person's ambitions are particularly effective in such tasks. It was impossible to know whether or not I would need him later but at least I felt that he could now be counted on.

Room 723 was halfway along the quiet corridor. I wandered up and down a few doors, making sure that all was deadly-dull normal. The usual noises of cable television and people talking on phones; nothing unusual. I went back to 723 and listened hard at the door – there was always the possibility that it was a twin or double room. Although I could hear nothing I rehearsed my "They've given me the wrong key again" exit line. To make that succeed I needed to act with confidence. Nothing is as suspicious as someone acting suspiciously. I put the key noisily into the lock, humming a tune. *Swan Lake*, I think. I entered panting and closed the door firmly behind me. Still humming happily I moved forwards four or five feet along the entranceway and found myself in a well-kept bedroom with no sign of its occupant. I turned my attention to the door. It was a standard self-locking type. With a simple extra turn to the right I was able to seal myself in.

The play would now run thus. The room occupant would return to the hotel and ask for his key. This would not be found initially. All the nearby key boxes would be checked for misfiling before it being declared that the key is definitely not there. All this while the receptionist will be doubting the guest. She knows all about business lunches, late breakfasts and so on; the numerous opportunities that a guest has to leave his key behind. More important, she knows about the type of people she is dealing with. They will never admit they are wrong. Therefore she knows that, regardless of the fate of the key, it will be insisted that it was left behind with the hotel. Furthermore, no well-trained receptionist would ever question the word of a guest publicly. At some point the spare key will be produced and the guest will promise to take extra care.

The occupant of 723 will then make his way up to the room and try the door, only to find that they key does not work. Why? Because the door is now locked from the inside. He will not be surprised. After all, they have already lost the first key and it is entirely in keeping with such incompetence that they would give him the wrong spare key. His irritated twisting and pushing of the door handle would be my alarm system. It would give me a clear three minutes, possibly even ten or more if the manager became involved. That was more than enough time. They would return and effortlessly secure entry. No sign of my being there would remain. Whatever was missing would only be noticed many hours, more likely days, later.

There was a briefcase and a suitcase in the bedroom. In the bathroom I found what I had been looking for – a razor. I immediately set about shaving. Lathering up, I realized how hungry I was. The room-service menu was, as is traditional, under the telephone. I phoned down for a club sandwich – and a bottle of wine. My drought was as pronounced as my whiskers. I went back to the bathroom. Shaving was not as painful as I had imagined it would be. The gooey moisturizer which had covered me from head to foot in the hospital had also been worked well into my bristles. Consequently they were very soft, although it still took me two attempts to get my face completely done. I raked further in the toiletry bag and found a pair of nail scissors. I used these to give myself a good haircut, lopping off about three fingers of growth all round. The difference in ten minutes was profound. I was newly gaunt, my cheekbones visible for the first time in living memory. I wouldn't have known me. Was this Patrick Robertson? No time to lose, though. I tidied up the sink area, flushing the hair away and wiping clean all surfaces. I sat on the bed. All the while I had been listening for the approach of footsteps, the turn of the handle. Then I heard someone coming down the corridor. They stopped outside the door. Two sharp raps. "Room service."

Excellent. I tiptoed to the door and undid the lock. I moved back into the bathroom, part-closing the door and turning on the shower.

I ducked back in and closed the door. I heard someone enter and walk to the bed, clinking slightly. They then left with a jaunty "Thank you." I jumped out, eager to get my prizes. There on the bed was a tray with a covered plate and a bottle of

Cabernet Sauvignon 1992, or something. The cork had been pulled and then lightly re-inserted. How quaint, I thought. I discarded the cork and filled the glass. It went down beautifully. I stared out of the window at the wonderful world that was there, my hand reaching absent-mindedly for the plate of sandwiches. Such saintly triangles so beautifully cut. Why was I being forced from this world that I love so much? What had I done wrong? Where had all the fairness gone? I poured myself some more wine in recompense. Who was going to take my place? What upstart would fill my shoes in hotel lobbies all over Southeast Asia? Oh what gross injustice! I supped at my glass and stared out at the dusty city. This was all so wrong.

I turned to look at the room again. While my luck was holding out I decided to have a shower. I don't hold with showers normally; such an indifferent attitude to overall health, as if it is only the exterior of a person which requires a daily rinse. Sustained immersion in a bath is the only method of total cleansing. However, on this occasion I knew that time was against me and that a succession of faint driplets of hot water would be all I could afford. I turned on the water and stood in silence for a moment until satisfied that I would still be able to hear the door handle being rattled. So assured, I scrubbed my tender skin gingerly, emerging not three minutes later as a better-smelling, indeed a simply better, person. Clean people are of course inherently superior to dirty ones. Having no mind to put on the rather rank clothing I had just taken off, I bustled into the bedroom in search of replacements, opening the suitcase on the bed. I soon had a pair of canvas trousers, a T-shirt, underpants and socks. Everything was about one size too big. The shoes were impossible to keep on and I was forced to return to the running shoes. Semi-formal dress and running shoes – I would simply have to pretend I was an American. I tucked in the T-shirt as best I could and found a belt which I did up tightly.

In my haphazard dress I was again aided by the fact of being a foreigner in Asia. Once the continental divide has been passed an amazing liberation of fashion mores occurs. Everyone is so transparently trying to maintain a business-like demeanor that simply attempting to wear a suit or jacket and trousers is considered passable. It does not matter if both are covered in dust, dripped on by various unidentified exotic sauces or piebald with sweat. It is the effort that matters. Thus my slightly disheveled appearance was the ideal guise. Attired in my customary tailor-made perfection, eyebrows would have been raised. Now I was just Joe Asia-Trip.

I finished the wine, checking one last time for anything that might be of use, then that everything had been replaced or cleaned up with absolute precision. The room key was left on the bathroom counter, to further fuel the guest's confusion. Maybe I did leave it here, he'll think, before throwing it in the bin and blaming the receptionist. Anything else? There wasn't, and I moved to the door, opening it slightly, then moving swiftly out. I laid the room service tray with empty bottle outside the next-door room. No hotel stay is complete without an "I didn't order that" complaint about the bill on departure.

The corridor seemed more threatening than before. Keen to get away, I headed for the lifts. I looked at the buttons and decided on "Up." Thankfully there was no lift-boy on this occasion.

I got out at the fourteenth floor – generally another non-event level – ambling around until I found a maid cleaning out a vacated room. As it was now well after midday there was a better chance that this room would not be required today. I noted the number, then went for a stroll around a few other floors. She was gone when I came back about thirty minutes later. I put my shoulder against the door, leaned into it, turned the handle and gave a strong heave. It opened quietly. Most people do not realize how easily a hotel room can be barged upon. I know, having been "rescued" on a number of occasions by hotel management. If the doors were genuinely difficult to get into a lot of money would be spent every year on replacing expensive locks and the like. There are more instances than might be imagined of guests losing first one, then two keys; guests lying comatose on the bathroom floor surrounded by cheap Chinese brandy; guests going loco and refusing to come out until "the monkeys have gone."

The room was entirely empty. I pushed the door shut. There was minimal damage to the mechanism and I was able to lock it once more. To be sure, I placed a chair against it. Suddenly the bed filled my every thought. Ripping off my new-found clothes, I pulled the sheets back, climbed in and was sucked down into the deepest of sleeps.

I stayed in that room for two nights, then found another, then another. Over this period I was able to build up a good-sized wardrobe. The laundry bags that people leave outside their rooms for collection proved highly productive, allowing me to put together an acceptable collection of clothes. Similarly, the rows of shoes to be polished yielded both a pair of black brogues and a pair of tan slip-ons. To top it off I snaffled a decent leather hold-all off a trolley when a bell-boy was inside a guest room, yapping for a tip.

As a guest I was able to take in the daily news reports, on BBC World and CNN principally, although the local English-language broadcasts were occasionally more informative. It was through all of these that I watched the gradual transition of my case, from one of kidnap to one of international mystery.

In the first twelve hours or so after my flight from the hospital the suspicion was that I had been kidnapped, then that I had fled in a psychologically damaged state. But as eyewitness accounts were put together things became less clear. The breakthrough came with the positive identification of Anthony Hislop in Bangkok. This time they used medical and dental records before flying Mr. and Mrs. Hislop and Emma-Jane over for an enormously tearful press conference.

Despite my best efforts, it was inevitable that I should at some point be discovered. My indiscriminate pillaging of each room's supplies would not have gone unnoticed. At every stop I would empty the mini-refrigerator entirely, luxuriate for hours in baths, spend hours lounging on the balcony. Reports of such occurrences, even evidence itself would naturally be put down by the management to the work of cunning staff on the take themselves. But sooner or later even the lowliest of cleaners will, eventually, be believed. I came to one day to find that the door to my room was being forced opened slowly forcing back the chair placed against it. I had taken to sleeping fully clothed, anticipating such an eventuality. Quickly I slid the balcony door open, then hopped into the bathroom. Just then the chair gave and two security guards and what looked like a house manager ran in. I nipped out as they leaned over the balcony, nodding curtly to the bemused-looking, lower-caste cleaner. She would probably receive some sort of citation in the monthly hotel-management report. Who knows, perhaps she might even have made Employee of the Month.

I made my way to the bank of elevators. The resolute demeanor of the attendant reminded me of the magnificent stone face maintained by the bellboy during my ex- wife's departure tantrum in the Brussels Sofitel. Having agreed to accompany her on a romantic weekend break, I felt I had done my bit. For most of the two days I allowed her free range over the quaint capital while I kept to my favored position in Les Waffles Lounge Bar. Had I understood that this mini-break was actually a "make or break" occasion, I might have joined her for a half hour or so of shopping. As it was the sight of me being taken up to the room in a rather dilapidated hotel-issue wheelchair tested her dignity too much. For the full ten-story ascension both I and the bellboy were treated to a random exploration of English swear-word usage with little evidence of standard grammar. Indeed, the entire stream of invective consisted of nouns, or nouns made into adjectives or verbs. It ended when the bellboy announced, "Ze Floor Ten." The doors opened and my wife fired me forward along the corridor. Her parting volley, set against the hiss of the closing door, was the last thing I ever heard from her, lawyers notwithstanding. My wheel-bound impact with the far wall proved less welcome.

I walked out of the lift without hesitation. No one had joined me on the way down, allowing adequate time to gather myself. The dutiful lift operator stared rigidly ahead as I repeated "I am Patrick Robertson" in increasingly strident tones, smoothing down my clothes and at the same time removing any trace of sweat on my palms. On a related point it is worth noting that crowded bars allow you to dispense with the drying of hands after urination. Simply be sure to gently place your palms fully on the backs of a couple of people as you make your way apologetically through. Always say "Excuse me" rather than "Thank you."

I strode purposefully past the potted plants and lounge seats, avoiding eye contact with the many floating staff. Turning the corner into the main hotel entrance lobby, my attention was caught by a newspaper on a coffee table. In one corner of the front page was a sketched portrait of myself as was; with beard and matted, thick, almost curly hair, much as appeared in the hospital the headline read: "BALLOON HUNT CONTINUES" Inside, the story made frighteningly clear that I was a ruthless thief, fraud, murderer and rapist. The real Anthony had, it reminded us, been discovered in Thailand and was now happily reunited with his family. He had explained how the balloon had been stolen from him. Police had later found two very decomposed and unidentifiable bodies in the rainforest – no mention of the other four. These persons were presumed to be victims of the same impostor, thankfully described as being either American or Canadian, who had surfaced in the balloon basket, claiming to be Anthony. Emma-Jane said the she had been raped by this "horrible, ugly thing," while Dr. Patel noted that hundreds of thousands of dollars of treatment had been lavished on him. The police suspected that he had now fled the country but that every effort was being made to secure his capture. Mr. Hislop was quoted as saying that he would never forget "those terrible beady eyes." I put the paper back on the table and walked calmly out into the swarming afternoon heat.

28. GOOD

I now have a home, only a few hours' walk from the climate-controlled luxury of the hotel. The Sisters of Mercy are well-known in Calcutta, although infamous may be a more appropriate term. Their center of operations, just another northeast of the central district, was located with the noisy assistance of a few locals, some of whom tagged along until it became clear that no coins would be forthcoming. Arriving shortly before dinner that night, I entered and began helping with preparations for the meal. None of the local workers questioned my right to be there, or the quality of my assistance. I have been here ever since.

Of course I never actually met Mother Teresa, although I did see her from time to time. She was a very busy person, what with Calcutta and world peace and everything. Like everyone else, though, I felt the difference in the air when she was around, which was often enough. Other people told me about her, too. The tales still continue, although it was as well to take each new one with a degree of skepticism. Merely to be associated with a fresh story of her divinity is an aspiration for some of the people who turn up here. This ambition tends to fuel imaginations. Undoubtedly her image lives on. For many it is better than the real thing as it is less likely to present contradictions.

Mother Teresa's spirit can be found in a number of the people working here but in particular with the nuns. They are resolute, each determined to help with cold-blooded happiness, each one a study of their erstwhile leader. The general helpers, of which I am one, are not quite so well-defined. There are a good many "lost causes" here, trying to work out a last, desperate remedy. It is in some respects a Foreign Legion for the well-meaning. The vast majority of people are those who think that being and working here is a good thing to be, a position that is difficult to argue with. At the same time this type of person doesn't seem to last very long; a typical stay is about three to four months. Over this period the enthusiasm for benign work is dulled, gradually replaced by a bitter, often naked, contempt for those in need. The poor, diseased and oppressed are a dreary bunch and it does not take a great deal of exposure to them to stir a significant level of disdain. Consequently Mother Teresa now has a healthy export business in poor-bashing liberal arts graduates. This does at least provide those of us who are more permanent with a regular harvest of books from the departing disillusioned. I did once try to point out to one of those leaving that being disillusioned, i.e., having an illusion removed, was a good thing, but he wasn't interested, simply throwing me his copy of *Les Misérables* and climbing into the truck to take him to the airport. He didn't even wave goodbye.

I have waved goodbye. I have waved goodbye to a large number of people who were dying. Holding their hand is one thing but it seems more human, more hopeful, to end with a wave of the hand. It does often produce a smile at the final moment. It sets the scene for the beginning of a journey.

Most do not die, though. Most get better. A large part of my time is taken up with these people. In doing so I have come to understand more clearly Mother Teresa's definitions of poverty. The first type is the lack of material things – mobile telephones, microwave ovens and the like. The second is the much more significant spiritual poverty. This is the absence of companionship, love, God. It is towards this latter impoverishment that our efforts are directed in the main.

Making people feel better is something I have just slipped into, with no more or less consciousness than I became a salesman. It does not make me feel any more worthwhile than selling did. Nor does it make me feel any worse. I do not miss being a salesman as such, although my disposition may well be affected by the fact that being a salesman is a road now closed. While anonymity is easy among the poorest of the poor, any attempt at a full-scale return to civilization would inevitably end in recognition. Even here I am careful to shave daily, grooming myself diligently and thus denying anyone a quick match with the hairy, bearded perpetrator of those crimes.

I do miss some of the old comforts. Painful as most of them were, the odd business lunch or dinner is a pleasant enough way to skip a large chunk of the day. Business itself – the humdrum talk of products and prices – is a more abstract absence.

Almost every second day or so I drop into a hotel to consult the Welcome board for conventions and the like. Such gatherings are always incredibly easy to gain access to and I could probably spend a lot of my time at them, but it's safer, I feel, to limit such excursions to two or three a month. On such days, though, I can sit among the crowd, listening to, and applauding, speaker after speaker on whatever arcane subject it is, then mingle quietly during the buffet, helping myself to all the passing wine I can. It's usually possible to borrow a newish shirt from one of our recent foreign arrivals, so looking the part is never a problem. Sometimes there's even a free bar. It's nice to feel the bite of a good dry martini or the slow glide of a Bloody Mary, particularly after a hot day with the wretched of the earth. To stand among the bespoke mini-palm trees, or wander round the pond of many carp, is a fine temporary relief. And sometimes, when I am feeling particularly undefined I will once more cheat my way into a couple of nights or so of five-star comfort. But for the most part I am to be found at the Sisters of Mercy. There are worse things to end up doing than good.

ABOUT THE AUTHOR

Brian Hennigan is a critically-acclaimed British novelist, director, and comedy producer. His plays, short stories, and novels including - *Patrick Robertson: A Tale of Adventure* - have been adapted, commissioned and broadcast on BBC radio. Hennigan's work has taken him around the globe, including teaching Shakespeare to graduate students at prestigious Lanzhou University in northwestern China, and Basic English to engineers at a TDK factory in rural Japan. His professional background includes senior marketing positions with Nissan Europe, Pringle of Scotland and The Macallan Malt Whisky. These days Hennigan lives in West Hollywood, where he is the business and producing partner of comedian Doug Stanhope.